Ascension Centennial
1907–2007
✢

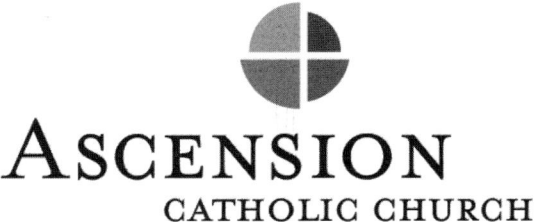

Ascension Centennial
1907–2007

THE
DONNING COMPANY
PUBLISHERS

Copyright © 2007 by Ascension Catholic Church

All rights reserved, including the right to reproduce this work in any form whatsoever without permission in writing from the publisher, except for brief passages in connection with a review. For information, please write:

The Donning Company Publishers
184 Business Park Drive, Suite 206
Virginia Beach, VA 23462

Steve Mull, General Manager
Barbara Buchanan, Office Manager
Pamela Koch, Senior Editor
Stephanie Danko, Graphic Designer
Derek Eley, Imaging Artist
Debbie Dowell, Project Research Coordinator
Scott Rule, Director of Marketing
Tonya Hannink, Marketing Coordinator

G. Bradley Martin, Project Director

Library of Congress Cataloging-in-Publication Data

Ascension centennial, 1907/2007.
   p. cm.
 ISBN 978-1-57864-460-5 (hard cover : alk. paper)
1. Ascension Catholic Church (Oak Park, Ill.)—History. 2. Oak Park (Ill.)—Church history. I. Donning Company Publishers.
 BX4603.O25A83 2007
 282'.7731--dc22
                                    2007032509

Printed in the United States of America at Walsworth Publishing Company

Contents

Preface	7
Mission Statement	8
Letter from Francis Cardinal George, O.M.I., Archbishop of Chicago	9
Letter from Father Larry McNally, Pastor	10
CHAPTER ONE *Father Thomas J. McDevitt, 1907–1936*	12
CHAPTER TWO *Monsignor William A. Cummings, 1937–1944*	28
CHAPTER THREE *Father Francis Ryan, 1944–1951*	36
CHAPTER FOUR *Monsignor John D. Fitzgerald, 1951–1973*	52
CHAPTER FIVE *Father Bernard White, 1973–1980*	70
CHAPTER SIX *Father Gerard T. Broccolo and Father Robert Cross, 1980–1988*	84
CHAPTER SEVEN *Father Francis C. Jenks, 1988–2003*	98
CHAPTER EIGHT *Father Lawrence R. McNally, 2003–Present*	118
CHAPTER NINE *The Centennial Year, 2006–2007*	132
Centennial Fund Donors	152

Preface

It has been our great pleasure to gather information for this book. We have had the opportunity to hear the stories of our parish—your stories—and to connect them with each other and with the facts as we knew them. We read sixty years worth of *Domes* and came to know the voices of their authors. In between the lines of announcements, of bowling scores and obituaries, of calls for volunteers and invitations to card parties, we could hear the voices of our own history. It has felt like eavesdropping, a surprisingly intimate encounter with the characters who played roles in our past. We wonder what happened to them as their own stories played out.

We are fortunate to have had some ready resources in our newly gathered archives. Intrepid Ascension historians before us produced books for the dedication of the church in 1929, the fortieth anniversary of the school in 1952, the dedication of the second school building in 1954, the fiftieth anniversary of the parish in 1957, and the fiftieth anniversary of the church in 1979! We have lifted material from those volumes shamelessly but not without checking sources against each other and against newspaper archives. Consequently, we have made some corrections in those old Ascension legends—and we suspect that when we write the book for the school centennial (2012), we will be correcting errors from this work! For all inevitable errors and omissions, we offer our apologies.

Many portions of this book were written by parishioners whose involvement at Ascension gave them a very particular expertise: Regina Kuehn, Pat McAnany, Mary McEnery, Christine Ondrla, Gina Orlando, and Jo Serio (who wrote her memories in 1990 and now sings with the heavenly choir). Thank you for your wonderful contributions.

Thank you to the Ascension Alumni Association of the 1990s; the work you did planted the seeds for this project and for others. Thanks, too, to all the parishioners and alumni who have sent pictures and stories to the parish over the years. Many thanks to Louise Snyder and Peg Zak, longtime parishioners and members of the centennial committee, for much of the legwork; their articles in *The Dome* throughout the centennial year were a source of inspiration, not to mention much information. Thanks to Bill Komala, who shares yet another gift with Ascension: he's a great photo archivist; to Keith Kalemba, who helped us get started with our recording project; to Sister Rosemary Meiman, OSU, for sharing treasures from the Ursuline Archives with us; to Dan Haley and Josh Hawkins of the *Wednesday Journal*, for allowing us to reprint their work.

The Centennial Book Committee
Celine Woznica (chair), Dan Dobruse, Claudia Hallissey, Lynn Fredrick, Vicky Tufano

The Centennial Committee
Donna Ioppolo (chair), Colleen Bracco, Tracy Brooker, Lynn Fredrick, Tom Gull, Neil Heskin, Linda Lewis, Fr. Larry McNally, Josie Mazzaia, Louise Snyder, Roger Vandervest, Celine Woznica, Peg Zak

The Centennial Photographers
Mary Beth Blatner, Bob Creed, Dottie Hetzel, Rich Hillengas, Ron Orzel, Marie Whittaker

Ascension Mission Statement

Ascension Parish in Oak Park is a Catholic community called to proclaim, to reflect on, and to live the Gospel. Our desire to follow Jesus inspires us to continue the rich traditions of our faith by supporting education for children and adults, celebrating the liturgical life of the community, and serving those in need within our parish and beyond. Following the example of Jesus, we value the diversity of gifts in all people, and all are welcome.

Ascension Catholic Church
808 South East Avenue
Oak Park, Illinois 60304
708.848.2703
www.ascensionchurch.com

ARCHDIOCESE OF CHICAGO

OFFICE OF THE CARDINAL

June 11, 2007

Dear Father McNally and Members of Ascension Parish,

Congratulations as you celebrate the centennial of the founding of your parish. During this historic year, I join you in giving praise and thanks to God who, generation after generation, helps His people to grow in holiness and builds up His Church.

On July 3, 1907, when your founding pastor Father Thomas McDevitt first rode the Garfield Park elevated train to the prairie land of south Oak Park and parts of what are now Berwyn and Forest Park, Catholics were few and not always welcome in that sparsely populated area. A century later, Ascension Parish has grown into a vibrant community of nearly 1900 families who are alive with the love and compassion of Christ and eager to invite others to join them as His disciples. Throughout the past hundred years, through prayer, sacrifice, service and celebration, you have sought to establish yourselves as a faithful presence, a social conscience and a caring neighbor, deeply rooted in Oak Park but also immersed in the life of the Universal Church and the world. Your traditions of reverent and beautiful worship, excellent Catholic education and faith formation, and dedication to social justice and care for the poor would, no doubt, make Father McDevitt proud, just as they make me grateful as your Archbishop.

As you build upon their faith and generosity of those who went before you, and as you continue to do the Lord's work in your community, I promise you my continuing prayers and count on the support of yours. May God bless you and those you love.

Sincerely yours in Christ,

Francis Cardinal George, O.M.I.
Archbishop of Chicago

155 East Superior • Chicago, Illinois 60611 • 312-751-8230 • FAX: 312-337-6379

Letter from Francis Cardinal George, O.M.I., Archbishop of Chicago

ASCENSION
May 2007

Dear Family of Ascension,

God's holy and good blessings on our Ascension Parish Family on this grand occasion of our 100th Anniversary. I personally am thrilled to be a part of this wondrous celebration. I thank you for welcoming me and for bringing me into your Family. I am so happy here, and I thank you.

My favorite definition of Church is "a meeting place between God and God's People." Thus, in our case, a meeting place between God and God's Family of Ascension. As Bishop McManus so wonderfully shared in his homily at the Golden Jubilee Mass, "This Church is our home and that is why we love it." In this home, so many wonderful and sacred prayer experiences happen. Indeed, it is our place, our home where we meet with God.

In our founding pastor's memoirs, Father Thomas McDevitt recalls the words Archbishop James Quigley told him when he was assigned to begin our Ascension Parish: "If you can not make a go of it in those vast prairies of wild, sweet clover, don't hesitate to come back. I will understand." Well, thank the Good Lord our God that Father McDevitt did not return back. Father McDevitt was a man of courage and determination, and above all, a man with a consuming love for his parish.

One hundred years later we can reflect on our parish as a sacramental Church.

Just think of the number of Baptisms celebrated where babies, children, teens, and adults were brought into the Family of God in the waters of Baptism, thus giving them the common name that we all share—Christian—and giving them the right to receive the other sacraments of our Church.

Just think of the number of First Holy Communions that have been received and celebrated, saying Amen to the Real Presence of the Lord in Eucharist as we eat the Bread of Life and drink from the Cup of Blessing.

Just think of the countless number of times the Sacrament of Reconciliations has been celebrated! We sacramentally celebrate the forgiveness of the Lord in our hearts. The word *reconcile* means "to look in the eye again." And because of this healing sacrament of God's Mercy, we can once again "look God in the eye."

Just think of the celebrations of Confirmation, the sacrament where we acknowledge the working of the Holy Spirit within our hearts, helping us to live out and share the gifts of that same Holy Spirit.

Just think of the many times the Sacrament of Marriage, where a man and woman give each other this sacrament of commitment, and thus two become one. In this sacrament, when love is not merely talked about but lived and shared, the *I* turns into the *We*.

Just think about the other sacrament of healing, the Sacrament of the Anointing of the Sick, where God's believers place their trust in God's healing hands, knowing that God is with them in their sickness. The sacred oil placed upon the forehead and hands is a sign that the healing Lord Jesus, who cures all our ills, is walking right them.

815 South East Avenue, Oak Park, Illinois 60304 phone: 708 848-2703

And then there the Sacrament of Holy Orders, which I feel so blessed to be called. On this 100th Anniversary, we can think about parishioners who have been ordained priests. We can think about parishioners who have been ordained deacons. We can think about the many priests who served our parish. But at the same time, we must also think about the women and men parishioners who have been professed into religious life. We can think the Ursulines and all the religious who have served here teaching us about God not only in word but also by their humble, sincere, and simple faith-lifestyle. We need to keep in prayer the need of an increase of vocation to the religious life, priesthood, permanent diaconate, and lay ministry.

On this grand occasion of our 100th Anniversary we thank Father McDevitt for not returning to Archbishop Quigley and for being consumed by his love for our Parish Family of Ascension.

The most important part of our parish life is the church where we celebrate daily Eucharist except for Good Friday. Eucharist is at the center of our parish life. I call to mind the verbs of the Eucharist: *gather, hear, offer, receive,* and *go*. Each of the days we *gather* as the Family of God, as the Family of Ascension to do what Jesus asked us to do, "in memory of me." We *hear* the Word of God, which brightens our hearts and minds as God speaks to us. As the gifts of bread and wine are processed up the aisle, we *offer* ourselves to our God, who loved us first and best by giving us Jesus Christ, God's greatest gift to us. And we *receive* back the Body and the Blood of Jesus Christ, saying "Amen," saying "I believe," saying "yes" in the act of bowing as well as in the saying of the word.

And then there is the *go*. You, my Family of Ascension, are so very good at this *go*. You live Eucharist so very well in your sense of compassion and kindness to the needy. You live Eucharist so very well with your sense of peace and justice. You live Eucharist so very well in terms of stewardship within our parish. You live Eucharist so very well with your many thoughtful words and deeds. "The Mass is ended, go now in peace with the Lord" and you, my Family of Ascension, are indeed peacemakers, daughters and sons of God.

I pray for you every day.

God's holy and good blessings on our Ascension Parish Family on this grand occasion of our 100th Anniversary.

With my love,

Father Larry McNally

Father Larry McNally
Pastor

P.S. See, I can write a parish letter without a pun or two.

CHAPTER ONE

Father Thomas J. McDevitt

1907–1936

Joseph Kettlestrings purchased the land between Harlem and Oak Park avenues and between Chicago and North avenues in 1837. James Scoville and Milton Nies purchased land to the south and east of Kettlestrings' and subdivided it in the 1860s. Saint Luke Church was founded in River Forest as a mission in 1865 and served all the Catholic families west of Chicago and east of the Des Plaines River.

In 1871, Chicago had a fire. In response to the fire, thousands of families who had to rebuild moved west. They settled first in the area known then as Ridgeland, now east Oak Park. Architects Seward Gunderson and Thomas Hulbert designed and began to develop the area south of Madison in 1906. Homes were purchased as quickly as they could build them, more than two hundred between 1907 and 1912. In 1870, the population of Oak Park was 500; thirty years later, it was 19,500. Many of the newcomers were Irish, mostly Catholic, and they needed a place to worship.

A New Parish

Archbishop James E. Quigley gave the commission to begin a parish in south Oak Park to the Reverend Thomas J. McDevitt. Father McDevitt was born in Belvidere, Illinois, on June 20, 1869. He attended Saint Viator College in Bourbonnais, Illinois, which had opened in 1865 and would close in 1937. His seminary studies were pursued at the Sulpician Seminary in Baltimore, Maryland, where Cardinal James Gibbons, the archbishop of Baltimore, ordained him on December 22, 1894. The earlier years of Father McDevitt's priesthood were spent as assistant at Our Lady of Mount Carmel, Saint Patrick, Saint Brendan, and Saint Columbkille parishes in Chicago.

When Father McDevitt arrived in Oak Park, the archdiocese had already purchased land for the parish and had begun to negotiate for temporary headquarters where he could say Mass. Father McDevitt named the new parish Ascension. It would serve the small Catholic population of eighty Catholic families who lived within the boundaries of the new parish: Austin Boulevard to the Des Plaines River, from Madison Street to Twenty-second Street. The diocese had purchased the land at East Avenue and Van Buren Street to build the parish campus, but there was much work to be done before any buildings could be erected.

At the same time, a parish to serve the Catholics in north Oak Park was being formed; the Reverend John J. Code would lead it. This parish, to be called Saint Edmund, met initially in a hall at Scoville Place, with land purchased at Pleasant and Oak Park Avenue for the eventual construction of the church.

Father McDevitt said his first Mass for the Ascension congregation in Shulte's Hall on Sunday, July 21, 1907, two weeks after he arrived in Oak Park. Shulte's was located on the southwest corner of

Ascension's first "church" at Scholte's Clubhouse on Scoville Avenue.

Harrison and Clarence. Even before Father McDevitt's arrival, the archdiocese had begun to negotiate for a larger, albeit still temporary, site for Father McDevitt to say Mass. The Phoenix Clubhouse was located at 641 S. Scoville, near the land already purchased for the Ascension campus. Mr. A. J. Flitcraft owned it.

A Misunderstanding

In a slight pamphlet called *The History of a Misunderstanding*, Mr. Flitcraft exposed the hubbub that ensued when it was learned that Catholics were interested in purchasing his property for a temporary church. Grace Episcopal Church had entered into negotiations to rent the clubhouse in the summer of 1907, as had representatives of the new Catholic parish. The conversation between Grace and the building's owner can be read in a series of letters between the principals, both of whom left the city for long stretches during the summer. Mr. Flitcraft makes public his correspondence with the Reverend E. V. Shayler, rector of Grace Episcopal Church, as a defense against the lawsuit eventually brought against him by Grace Church. The dispute was this: Grace Church began to use the clubhouse for meetings in September of 1907. Reverend Shayler never signed the lease that was sent him in August of that year and was late paying the rent for the three months that Grace used the building. Mr. Flitcraft sold the building out from under him. Reverend Shayler sued and lost.

The South Oak Park Station, 1907. Photo courtesy of the Historical Society of Oak Park and River Forest.

The little nugget of the story that led to Reverend Shayler's notoriety in the matter is contained in his letter to Mr. Flitcraft dated July 19, 1907. At the time of this letter, Father McDevitt had been in Oak Park for less than two weeks and had conducted at least one meeting of his future flock at the Phoenix Clubhouse. Reverend Shayler had just learned that his negotiations with Mr. Flitcraft were not without competition, and that the competitors are Catholic.

> *[In the 1930s], mice were running around the school rooms. We would shoo them up the radiators.*
>
> ✢ Pat Cullen

> Without disparagement or prejudice I am sure you can see that it will be better for you, for the property, for the neighborhood, for Oak Park, if we use it for Grace Church than if the R.C.s

Chapter One: Father Thomas J. McDevitt

[Roman Catholics] get it. You know the quality of their people and one glance at a used parochial school or public building of theirs will tell you what would happen to your building and neighborhood if they lease it.

We can assume, in charity and from the vantage point of one hundred years later, that Reverend Shayler wrote out of frustration and not out of personal prejudice. Catholics, however, were generally not welcome in Oak Park. Saint Edmund Parish also met with some resistance when they were preparing to build; John Farson, a leading Oak Park citizen, helped them. The home he had built for his family, at the intersection of Pleasant Avenue and Home Avenue,

Parishes Formed

Plans for organizing two Catholic parishes in Oak Park were brought to a head during the past week. Temporary places of worship have been secured pending the erection of church edifices, and the work of enlisting the Catholics of the village in support of each parish is well under way. Oak Park has been without a Catholic church since its foundation. The people of that creed have worshipped at the River Forest or Austin churches. The rapid influx of people of that denomination into the village, and particularly into south Oak Park, with its lack of north and south transportation facilities to convey the residents to either outside parish is said to have been primarily responsible for the appeals made to Archbishop Quigley for the formation of an Oak Park parish and the appointment of a pastor.

The archbishop accordingly divided the village into two parishes, one lying south of Madison Street between Harlem Avenue and Austin Avenue, the other situated between Madison and Chicago Avenue and Cuyler and Harlem Avenues.

. . . The Reverend Thomas J. McDevitt, assistant rector of St. Columbkille's church, on the northwest side of Chicago, has been appointed pastor. Rev. McDevitt was for thirteen years a Baltimore clergyman and for a shorter time assistant at the South Englewood church in Chicago. He is said to be a forceful speaker and an orator of no mean ability. He was present at the organization meeting held Thursday evening at the Flitcraft clubhouse on South Scoville Avenue at which thirty Catholic families were represented. It was decided to negotiate for a lease of the clubhouse as a temporary place of worship. There will be no service there on Sunday, July 14, but a meeting of the ladies of the parish will be held at 3:00 p.m. On Monday evening a meeting of the men will be held at the same place.

Excerpted from *The Oak Leaves*
Saturday, July 13, 1907

CHRISTMAS OFFERING, 1910
ASCENSION PARISH
OAK PARK, ILL.

CLARENCE AVE.
- 941 Mrs. M. Callahan .. $1.00
- 941 Master J. Callahan .25
- 945 E. J. Callahan .25
- 1112 F. Helle 2.00
- 945 Mr. and Mrs. F. J. Labree 5.00
- 619 Mrs. M. Lee 1.00
- 518 M. Purcell 1.00
- 518 Jno. Purcell Jr. 2.00
- 518 Mr. Jno. Purcell Sr. 2.00
- 941 Mrs. W. J. Stalba 1.00
- 941 W. J. Stalba 2.00
- 619 A. E Lee 1.00

CLINTON AVE.
- 858 Mrs C. Nelson 3.00
- 724 James C Barry 20.00
- 733 Mr and Mrs. J. Einhorn 10.00
- 800 Margaret McMahon 2.00
- 624 James J. Monahan 5.00
- 624 John A Monahan 5.00
- Dr. Keefe 1.00

CUYLER AVE.
- 831 D. Bouchard 3.00
- 831 Lewis C. Bouchard 1.00
- 644 Mrs. Dittman 1.00
- 1141 Albert Schmidt 2.00
- 642 Mr. O. St. John 1.00

EAST AVE.
- 620 M. Brahany 1.00
- 620 A. Brahany 5.00
- 735 J. J. Brown 2.00
- 635 Mrs. M. Clark 2.00
- 846 Fretz 1.00
- 846 Leo A. Fretz 1.00
- 1023 Edward Kain 2.00
- 1041 Chas. W. Myers 2.00
- 1023 Mrs Sullivan 1.00
- 1160 Jno. E Fitzgerald 2.50

ELGIN AVE.
- 913 Matthew Brown 2.00
- 842 Mr. J. Conser 1.00
- 842 Mrs. C. Hensel 1.00
- 1021 B. W. Schaefer 2.00
- 829 Mr. M. Small 2.00

ELMWOOD AVE.
- 600 J. E Brennan 5.00
- 600 S. Brennan 1.00
- 835 Mrs. Jas. T. Brown 1.00
- 718 T. F. Cummings 10.00
- 518 Anita Genschow 1.00
- 725 A. Larner 1.00
- 425 Rebbeca Mason 1.00
- 425 Margaret E. Mason 1.00
- 601 Veronica M. McCarthy 5.00
- 829 A. T. Murphy 5.00
- 614 Mrs. H. S. Nelson 2.00
- 530 Cecilia O'Connor 2.00
- 618 Mrs E. G. Purkhiser 3.00
- 618 John S. Reynolds 10.00
- 532 Clement Savage 1.00
- 532 Mrs L. J. Savage 2.00
- 530 Mrs. M. J. Ward 5.00
- 838 Mrs. A. Doyle 2.00

- 732 Mrs. F. L. Merrill 1.00
- 532 Dr. Savage 2.00

EUCLID AVE.
- 624 Mrs. E. Barrett 2.00
- 624 Wm. Bosley 2.00
- 1028 Daisy Cooney .05
- 1028 Stella Cooney 1.00
- 1011 James A. Foy and Family 5.00
- 1028 Mrs. O'Karlss 5.00
- 1034 Maguire 2.00
- 1146 Mrs. J. H Maxwell 2.00
- 1017 J. P. McParland 10.00
- 1017 Mr. and Mrs. H. J. Spencer 5.00
- 1017 Mr. Thos. Spencer 1.00
- 1017 Mary Spencer 1.00
- 1017 H. J. Spencer .25
- 1017 Martin G. Spencer .25

GRACE AVE.
- 621 Thos. Mevers 1.00
- 517 Mrs F. Rohl 2.00
- 534 M. Wheeler 3.00

GUNDERSON AVE
- 539 John Brennan 5.00
- 539 Mrs. Mary Brennan 5.00
- 539 M Brennan 1.00
- 614 Mrs. G. S. Fairman 2.00
- 634 Nora Hyde 1.00
- 823 L. F Maddock 10.00
- 710 Mr. Alex Meyers 2.00
- 734 Mr and Mrs. Thos. Roch 5.00
- 709 Chas. Roche 1.00
- 734 John A. Roch .25
- 734 Wm. Roch .25
- 724 C. F Ravenstein 5.00
- 734 Julia E. Roch 1.00

HARRISON ST.
- 7000 Mr. and Mrs. A. F. Adams 2.00
- 7000 John Ensweiler 2.00
- 7000 Mrs. F. Uthoff 1.00

HARRISON PL.
- 6602 C. J. McCarthy 5.00

HARVEY AVE.
- 534 Miss Carse 1.00
- 1129 Miss E. D. Elkins 1.50
- 882 Mrs. F. F. O'Brien 1.00
- 882 Gertrude O'Brien 1.00

HIGHLAND AVE.
- 834 Evea Joy 1.00
- 884 Kathryn Joy 1.00
- 725 J. Lusk 2.00
- 828 Mrs. Patterson 5.00
- 729 Marion Quigley 2.00
- 725 Mrs. C. Lusk 1.00

HUMPHREY AVE.
- 836 Mr. and Mrs E. V. Gill 2.00
- 808 Evelyn Herbert 1.00
- 808 J. L. Herbert 5.00
- 1165 C. McCarthy and Family 5.00

HOME AVE.
- 1139 Mrs. B. Kelly and Family 5.00
- 1101 Mrs. J. J. Dowling 2.00
- 1019 L. H. Malone 5.00
- 1047 Olga Merk .75
- 1047 Joseph Merk .50
- 1137 C. A. H. Miller 2.00
- 625 Mary Shea 1.00
- 625 Mrs. M. Shea 1.00
- 625 Margaret Shea 1.00

KENILWORTH AVE
- 721 C. M. Bentley 10.00
- 819 Mrs. Wm. Bromann 1.00
- 1164 Mrs. A. J. Coty 1.00
- 508 Mary Kean 2.00
- 508 J. E. Simpson 5.00
- 508 Miss May Simpson 1.00
- 1164 Catherine Smith 2.00
- 1164 Margaret Smith 2.00
- 940 Mrs. J. F. Wellmer 1.00

LOMBARD AVE.
- 818 John Coghlan 1.00
- 1155 Mr. F. Finn 1.00
- 1151 Mrs. A. Shanley 1.00

LYMAN AVE.
- 808 J W. Best 1.00
- 544 D. Gallagher 5.00
- 637 E. W. Johnson 1.00
- 1017 Thos. Mahoney 1.00
- 808 W. H. Keller 1.00
- 553 J. L. Stapleton Jr. 1.00

MAPLE AVE.
- 1010 Mrs. C. C. O'Neill 2.00
- 530 Mrs. J. T. McBride 5.00

OAK PARK AVE.
- 1124 T. W. Breen 1.00
- 737 Jno. Donahue 5.00
- 808 Peter Donlan 3.00
- 736 Mrs. Geo. Schrage 1.00
- 736 Anna H. Schrage 1.00
- 507 Joseph Stehle 5.00
- 507 Ed. Stehle 1.00
- 809 Miss N. V. Bisarek .50

SCOVILLE AVE.
- 537 Miss A. Breen 5.00
- 522 Mr. J. Carmichael 5.00
- 641 Julia Carroll 5.00
- 1031 Josephine Hoch .50
- 634 Winifred Kilfeather 1.00
- 634 Miss A. Kilfeather 1.00
- 634 T. Kilfeather 5.00
- 634 Genevieve Kilfeather 1.00
- 742 Thos. J. O'Brien 5.00
- 705 P. Shea 5.00
- 709 Mrs. Jas. Teal 1.00
- 825 Mrs. E. A. Vail 5.00
- 801 Thos. S. Williams 10.00
- 640 George Mayo 5.00

SIXTY-FOURTH AVE.
- 759 Wm. J. Becker 2.00
- 849 Jas. M. Feron 3.00

- 733 P. J. Honan 2.00
- 721 Mrs. J. T. Hyde 1.00
- 825 Phoebe Maether 1.00
- 531 Thos. McQuade 2.00
- 839 C. Strenning 1.00
- 835 Mrs. M. Strenning 1.00
- 835 Mr. E. Walsh 2.00
- 835 Mrs. M. Walsh 2.00

WENONAH AVE.
- 912 F. A. Deppen 2.00
- 912 Jennie Deppen .25
- 912 Mary Deppen .25
- 912 J. L. Deppen 3.00
- 912 Mrs. Jas. Deppen 2.00
- 701 Charlotte Haberkorn .50
- 1022 P. E. Myers 2.00
- 929 F. Myers 3.00
- Thos. O'Connor 20.00
- 1138 Mr. Powers 1.00
- 524 Margaret Shine 10.00
- J. A. Haberkorn 20.00

WESLEY AVE.
- 1031 C. Arnum 5.00
- 1002 Clarence Bartels .50
- 1002 Mrs. F. H. Bartels 2.00
- 1002 Hazel Bartels 1.00
- 936 Marie Foley 2.00
- 1152 Stephen F. Foy 2.00
- 1152 M. and K. Foy 5.00
- 640 Mahon 2.00
- 932 Miss Jane Rutledge 2.00
- 1109 Misses L. and M. Sammon 2.00
- 706 E. Sheehan 5.00
- 735 Mr. and Mrs. J. P. Sheridan 5.00
- 937 Jas. M. Sheridan 2.00
- 706 M. and C. Sheehan 10.00
- 932 M. J. Wheeler 1.00
- 1023 Mrs. Wison 2.00
- 615 A. A. Winter 5.00
- 1160 John J. Enright 3.00

TAYLOR AVE.
- 803 Jos. Kramer 2.00
- 736 Mrs. Sophia Lardinois 1.00
- 736 Mr. and Mrs G. M. Masters 5.00
- 817 M. J. Slavik 2.00

TWELFTH ST.
- 1235 Mrs. J Burke 5.00

DUNLOP AVE.
- 1134 Mrs. L. Koeplle 1.00

MISCELLANEOUS
- Mrs. Wm. Loechel 1.00
- Miss. Gillan 2.00
- Mr. Henry McAlear 1.00
- Mrs. Dorathy Murray 1.00
- Cash 2.00

All errors and omissions cheerfully corrected.

T. J. McDevitt
PASTOR.

Memo: To Monsignor Fitzgerald
The total of the Christmas offering in 1910 = $577.25
The total of the Christmas offering in 1956 = $14,186.50

Ascension's church was located on the second floor of the school building from 1911 until 1929.

is now known as Pleasant Home, the current site of the Oak Park Historical Society. Roberta Savler Lysaght wrote in a piece for the Oak Park Bicentennial, "I remember my Jewish mother's recounting with amusement that, as a newcomer to Oak Park, she was asked by a Protestant neighbor, 'What are we going to do about all the Catholics that are moving in?'"

Establishing Roots

Father McDevitt was much loved by the Ascension community. He came to south Oak Park alone and worked alone gathering his flock until an assistant, Father Bernard Brady, joined him in 1911. One of Father McDevitt's first moves, within days of his arrival in

Oak Park, was to invite the women of the parish to begin the Altar and Rosary Society. In fact, an article in the *Oak Leaves* dated Saturday, July 13, 1907, announced that no Mass would be held the following day but that the ladies would meet at 3:00—one week before the first Mass was celebrated. The first president of Altar and Rosary was Mrs. J. J. Quinlan.

Father McDevitt began the construction of the school in 1911 and, in the summer of 1912, asked Mother Paul of the Ursuline Mother House in Springfield, Illinois, to send nuns to teach the children. Father McDevitt had visited several orders before the Ursulines, but none of them had been able to meet his need. But when he told the story of great interest for a school among his parishioners but very little money and significant debt, Mother Paul simply asked, "How many sisters do you need and when do you need them?"

Registration for school took place the day after the nuns arrived, and school started immediately. Two hundred and forty children arrived when classes began in fall 1912, some of them high school aged and in need of a place to board. The Ursulines made arrangements to meet the needs of all the children.

The school building included a parish hall in the lower level (it would become the Pine Room in 1944 after a remodeling led by Father Ryan), the church and some classrooms on the middle floor, and more classrooms and the convent on the top floor. The church was located at the south end of the second floor. Students who attended Ascension School in its first decade recall having to genuflect when they passed through the

> *Our family moved to Oak Park in April of 1919. My parents and three sisters were climbing the front stairs to attend the nine o'clock Mass. Father McDevitt was standing at the top of the stairs and asked us where we were going. My father said we were there to attend Mass. "No adults," he said, "This is the children's Mass." So we all went home.*
> ✢ *Verna Schwenke Frillman*

Altar of church in the school building.

Chapter One: Father Thomas J. McDevitt

The Class of 1938 in seventh grade. Photo courtesy of Jim Sender (JS), class of 1938.

The construction of Ascension Church, 1929.

through the stairwell next to the altar on their way between classes. Archbishop Quigley formally dedicated the building on December 23, 1912. Mass was said by Monsignor Legris of Saint Viator's College; Armand Crabbe, a singer with the Chicago Opera, sang; nine hundred people attended.

With the church and school built, the Phoenix Clubhouse became the social center for the parish. Bowling alleys and billiards helped keep young men in the neighborhood from "the very questionable pleasures and amusements" that were available to them on the east boundary of Oak Park.

That same year Father McDevitt ordered the construction of a red brick building large enough to house parish offices and five priests. The rectory originally sat at the corner of East Avenue and Van Buren Street and faced north. It was moved to 815 S. East Avenue in 1929 to make way for the construction of the church.

Within three years, the school population had grown enough that the third floor of the school, which was then the covent, was needed for classrooms. The parish had to find other living quarters for the Ursulines. Father McDevitt moved them into the Phoenix Clubhouse on Scoville Avenue until better arrangements could be made. The better arrangements came in the purchase of the two homes directly across East Avenue from the rectory. A bridge was built to connect the second floors of the two homes; it became known as "the bridge of sighs."

> *I was born in January 1911. At that time, Father McDevitt would say Mass in the back room of Vogel's Tavern at Harrison Street and Harlem Avenue to accommodate the parishioners who lived too far from the church on Scoville Avenue. . . . [A]fter closing up on Saturday night, Mr. Vogel would have the back room of the tavern, with the family entrance and the family trade, cleaned up, the tables neatly lined against the wall and chairs placed in orderly rows for Sunday Mass. So, on a cold, blizzardy Sunday, I was taken as a babe in arms to Vogel's [Tavern] where Father McDevitt baptized me and welcomed me to his little flock.*
>
> ✦ *Genevieve Karthold Flanagan*
> *Class of 1925*

Gertrude and Agnes Shea, and Lillian and Leona Ann Mayo, 1914.

The students of Ascension School donated the money for the statue of Jesus that stands atop the dome of Ascension Church.

Virginia Humble, Marjorie Hardin, Mary Miller, Frances Craig, and Lorraine Ward from the class of 1933. Photo courtesy of Winifred Halvorsen Soucie (WHS), class of 1933.

Social Life

The younger women of the parish formed the Young Ladies' Sodality. In 1925, fourteen members of Sodality formed the Tivedan Dramatic Club. Under the direction of Mrs. Walter Caron, the club produced musical comedies to entertain the community and to help raise money to build the church. Geraldine Schwenke Brons wrote in 1979 of her memories of this project: "Father McDevitt was our pastor at the time, so I took the last part of his name, reversed it, then added the first and last letters of Ascension and the result was Tivedan. The group liked the name since it had a special meaning to us; it embodied our pastor and our parish."

The Tivedan Dramatic Club was the beginning of Ascension's dramatic bent. The children performed for appreciative audiences as often as possible. An Irish operetta, *Bits of Blarney*, was sold out for a two-night run. The *Oak Leaves* reported that the children, "with sweet old melodies, gladdened the heart and thrilled the soul." In the years to come, parishioners of all ages would perform in various productions.

The parish became the center of family life as early as the second decade of its existence. The Altar and Rosary Society held card parties; the Sodality held dances. Twice a year, the parish held bazaars that included a children's carnival and evening entertainment and raffles for the adults. All the money collected became part of the fund for building a church.

Building the Church

In November 1928, the archdiocese received a building permit to break ground for the construction of the church. The cost was projected at $235,000. The rectory was moved from its original location facing Van Buren Street, and the cornerstone for the church was laid on Easter Sunday, 1929. The church was designed by the Chicago architect firm of Meyer and Cook and built by the Mutual Construction Company. The Italianate design, with a ninety-foot dome and a mission tile roof, made Ascension "one of the most beautiful buildings in Oak Park," according to the *Chicago Tribune*.

Ascension, Oak Park, Will Mark a Double Jubilee

✠

The parishioners of Ascension parish will unite with their beloved pastor, the Rev. T. J. McDevitt, LL.D., in commemorating a double event—his silver anniversary as a pastor of a parish and the silver anniversary of the founding of this well-known Oak Park parish. A full week will be given to rejoicing and devotion.

On Sunday, October 23, the reverend jubilarian will be celebrant of a Solemn High Mass. The sermon on this occasion will be preached by the Rev. Ambrose Grissin, O.S.M., professor of English at Mater Dolorosa Seminary, Hillside, Ill. On Monday, October 24, solemn Requiem High Mass will be celebrated for all deceased members of the parish. On the evening of the same day, a parish dinner arranged by the Altar and Rosary society and the Young Ladies' Sodality will be given in the parish hall. On Tuesday evening, an entertainment sponsored by the Holy Name Society will be furnished. The children will rejoice with their pastor on Wednesday afternoon. On the evenings of Wednesday, Thursday, and Friday, October 26, 27, and 28 at 8:00 there will be a triduum in honor of St. Jude conducted at the new shrine in Ascension parish.

The Rev. Father McDevitt was born in Belvidere, Ill., June 20, 1869. He attended St. Viator College, Bourbonnais, and his seminary course was pursued at the Sulpician Seminary in Baltimore, Md. Father McDevitt was ordained on December 22, 1894, by the late Cardinal Gibbons in Baltimore. The earlier years of his priesthood were spent as assistant at Our Lady of Mount Carmel, St. Patrick's, St. Brendan's and St. Columbkille parishes. In 1907, McDevitt was commissioned to found Ascension parish, and there he has labored zealously to build a strong and spiritually healthy congregation. The crowning event of his career was realized in June 1930 when his Eminence Cardinal Mundelein officiated at the dedication of the beautiful new Italian Romanesque church of Ascension parish located at 815 South East Avenue. The edifice is one of the most attractive in the village and parishioners rejoice with their pastor in the completion of this beautiful House of God. The structure was designed by Meyer and Cook.

The dome was topped with a fifteen-foot statue of Jesus, contributed by the children of the parish. Sister Magdalen Fearon, a member of the Ascension class of 1932 who joined the Ursulines and returned to teach at Ascension, remembers one fundraising activity: "The school children brought our lunches to school each day—and then we sold them to each other for pennies for the church."

Dear Father Mac

Father McDevitt's leadership built the original Ascension building on Clarence and Van Buren, opened the school, and built the

Of the class of 1938, standing, from left, Bill Quirk, Charles Singer, Dennis Crowley, Robert Martin, and Phil Cagney; seated, from left, Bill Heckman and Bob Link. (JS)

Mother Catherine taught eighth grade at Ascension School and was a favorite among her pupils. (Photo 1938, JS)

Mother Bernardine taught fifth and sixth grades. (Photo 1932, WHS)

Father McMahon was the spiritual and sports director for Ascension. (Photo 1933, WHS)

Father McGovern, curate. (Photo 1933, WHS)

Kenneth Williams and Jack Mulholland, class of 1933. (WHS)

church. In memories shared by parishioners for books commemorating other Ascension anniversaries, he is universally referred to as "beloved" and "dear Father Mac."

The Golden Jubilee Book, published at the fiftieth anniversary of the dedication of the church, includes this memory from 1936 shared by Ila Bourgeois:

> It was a beautiful autumn afternoon. The Altar & Rosary regular monthly meeting was in session in the school hall. Escorted by his faithful chauffeur (Bill Dempsey), Father McDevitt came through the back door. Everyone stared for a moment, absolutely speechless. The once portly "Father Mac" was thin, emaciated, care-worn—his one arm in a sling. He told us to sit, but he remained standing in his characteristic commanding attitude. He spoke briefly. No one present would ever forget his well-prepared address.
>
> "It is with great effort that I come to you today. I was determined to come to you—you have heard me say repeatedly that the Altar & Rosary is the backbone of any parish. Because of the Altar & Rosary's loyalty

> *The Shea family moved to Oak Park in 1908. We lived at 705 S. Scoville Ave. Many in our family went to Ascension School. . . . The church was on the first floor and the school on the second floor of the present school building. . . . In our eighth grade we had my sister as a teacher, Sister Miriam Shea. Of course, guess who received the important part in the eighth grade play? None other than myself. Politics pays off.*
>
> ☩ *Marge Shea Nichol*
> *Class of 1925*

Chapter One: Father Thomas J. McDevitt

Reverend Mother Borgia taught several grades and was the fourth principal of Ascension School. (Photo 1932, WHS)

and hard work, we now have our great parish and excellent school, our beautiful new church with everything in it. I shall not be with you much longer; I have a request to make of you. I know that you will carry it out. When God calls me, I want no pompous funeral rites. I ask only of my loyal Altar & Rosary ladies that they will form in small groups and all during my wake, day and night as I lie in the church, they will keep the Rosary going for me. After my Funeral Mass, I want to be buried with my family in the McDevitt plot. Thank you."

In a very few weeks, on Thanksgiving Day at 10:30 p.m., Bill was helping Father remove his shoes. Suddenly, Father fell backward on the bed. He had gone to God. His wishes were carried out by the Altar & Rosary ladies, eight at a time. At night from 11:00 p.m. to 7:00 a.m., the Holy Name men kept the Rosary going. He is buried in the McDevitt family plot. ✠

Ascension Study Club Begins Activities for 1934–35 Season

✠

Ascension Study Club, now entering its second season of activity, has announced plans for a series of lectures during the winter months. The opening lecture by the Rev. Louis DeCelle, chaplain at Mercy Hospital, was given November 7 on the subject "Fascism." Fr. DeCelle introduced the study club idea at St. Thomas the Apostle Church while an assistant there, and its work for Catholic Action became widely known. The lectures of Ascension Study Club, which is under the direction of the Rev. Bernard Burns, are only part of its activities. At the regular meetings, which are held at Ascension hall on the second and fourth Wednesdays of the month from October to June, an interesting discussion is entered into by members on some popular subject. Last season, the topics included Catholic Education, the Catholic Press, and the Family. The discussion on the Catholic Press brought about an agreement among the members to foster support of the *New World*. Another practical result was the subscription for Catholic magazines and the procuring of Catholic books for the South Branch of the Oak Park Public Library, which is in Ascension parish. The first topic to be discussed this year will be the social condition of the world and the remedies advocated by the Holy Father. This discussion will take place at the regular meeting on the second Wednesday of November. All adult members of Ascension and the neighboring parishes are invited to the lectures and to attend the meetings of the study club.

The first graduating class of Ascension School.

Two houses connected by a bridge served as the third convent for the Ursuline Sisters.

Chapter One: Father Thomas J. McDevitt

CHAPTER TWO

Monsignor William A. Cummings

1937–1944

After nearly thirty years of vision, leadership, and pastoral care, Father McDevitt left behind a vibrant parish with a beautiful church and an active school. Immediately following Father McDevitt's death, Cardinal Mundelein named Monsignor William A. Cummings the second pastor of Ascension.

Before becoming a priest, Monsignor Cummings had experienced life in the business world, and he brought those skills to his ministry. When Catholic Charities of Chicago was founded in 1917 to assist parishes in meeting the needs of the poor in their communities, he became its first director.

Monsignor Cummings' arrival at Ascension came as the United States and the rest of the world were emerging from the Great Depression. His work in Catholic Charities had touched him deeply. He knew the reality of the lives of the poor, and he understood what it took for ordinary people to make a living, pay for a home, and support a family.

It was understandable, then, that when this quiet man discerned the need to build another building, he moved ahead with caution. The burgeoning school enrollment had already displaced the Ursuline Sisters from their original quarters on the top level of school building. They were now residing in two houses on the southeast corner of East Avenue and Van Buren Street that were connected by a second-story passageway. It was clear that this arrangement was inadequate. A new convent was needed. With considerable hesitation, he presented the problem to the people, asking their guidance and direction. He found his parishioners solidly behind him, enthusiastic in their support of his proposal to build a new convent. As a matter of fact, the fund drive was oversubscribed. Under Monsignor's watchful eye, the convent was built in 1939.

World War II

The year 1939 also saw the beginning of the Second World War. Hitler had invaded Poland. Britain and France declared war. The U.S. economy began to recover as American industry filled orders from Europe for arms and war equipment, but the United States remained neutral until December of 1941, when Pearl Harbor was attacked.

Ascension, like all American communities, became involved in the war effort. Women went to work to fill the jobs the men had to leave to go to war. Meat, sugar, shortening, canned goods, shoes, gasoline, and tires were rationed. Family Victory Gardens provided fresh produce, which was in short supply. Adults and children alike bought government savings bonds and stamps to support the war, sometimes a dime or a quarter stamp at a time, until they reached $18.75 in stamps, which could be exchanged for a $25.00 bond. There were air-raid drills in the school and first-aid classes in eighth grade.

Many homes in the parish had flags with blue stars in the windows for their sons and daughters in the military. Some homes had gold-star flags, indicating that the loved one had died in service to the country.

In the Archdiocese of Chicago and throughout the country, Our Lady of Sorrows Novenas became a weekly practice

Monsignor Cummings laying the cornerstone for the new convent.

Graduating class of 1937.

for many Catholics. In the handwritten book of Mass announcements for Ascension is this announcement for Quinquagesima Sunday (the Sunday before Lent began) of 1943:

> The Sorrowful Mother Novena is sponsoring a crusade dedicated to Victory in 1943. The Crusade starts at the Novena Services on Friday, March 12th. Novena services every Friday at 4 and 8 o'clock.

Ordinary Parish Life

Even though the war was in the background of everything, parish life proceeded with some sense of normalcy. There were processions, May Crownings, and First Communions (with little clickers that the Sisters used to signal when to genuflect,

It was a beautiful summer day in 1939 when young Father John Loftus knocked on our door. He was taking a census for Ascension Parish. Father asked my mother why her school-aged children weren't attending Ascension. Eventually, four of seven daughters did graduate. So began my love of faith and Ascension, due to the exceptional priests and extraordinary Ursuline nuns. To this day, I am still influenced and guided by their teachings.

✝ *Norine Kresich Slott*
Class of 1942

The new convent, 1939. Note the Carron house north (left) of the convent; it was demolished in 1963.

stand, or sit). At school, there were spelling bees, mission banks, basketball, and, next to the school, Mrs. Quinlan's candy, milk, and school supplies store.

The Apostle of Charity

Even though he was a reserved man, Monsignor Cummings became more and more attached to his flock as they became more and more attached and devoted to him. He tended to his parish with devotion. He made the rounds of the parish buildings almost daily, watching for signs of structural weaknesses and supervising tuck pointing, painting, and other necessary repairs. He would hand out the report cards at the school. From his own limited funds came Christmas parties, picnics, and other treats for the school children, and awards to the graduates.

Convent refectory (dining room).

Convent Construction

✢

Ascension Church, Van Buren Street and East Avenue, Oak Park, Ill., is erecting an $84,000 convent on East Avenue opposite the church building. The new convent is being built in the Spanish Mission style and will consist of two stories and an English basement with tannish-yellow brick and limestone trimming. It will contain twenty-five rooms, providing accommodations for nineteen Sisters of the Ursuline Order. The new building is expected to be ready for occupancy by the middle of October.

The New World
Newspaper of the Archdiocese of Chicago
July 14, 1939

Construction of parish convents will mark the summer activities of two Catholic churches in the Chicago area, it was announced by their pastors this week. Ascension Church, Van Buren Street and East Avenue, Oak Park, is erecting an $84,000 convent on East Avenue opposite the church building....

Although Ascension Church is of the Byzantine form of architecture, the new convent is being built in the Spanish Mission style. It will be marked by simplicity and plainness of detail, according to the pastor, Msgr. W. A. Cummings, and will be L-shaped, with a patio, or open courtyard, in the rear, which will contain a rock garden. To the north of the patio there will be a cloister along the outside of the basement, partly below the ground level.

The convent will consist of two stories and an English basement, and will be built of a tannish-yellow brick with limestone trimming. It will contain 25 rooms, providing accommodations for sisters of the Ursuline order outside the parish, who may be there on temporary visits. There are nineteen sisters enrolled in the parish.

The approach to the convent will be terraced to take care of the elevation above the sidewalk level, and the same motif in one of the three church arches across the street will be reproduced in the entrance to the building. The music rooms and the large recreation room will be located in the basement, while the community room and chapel, facing the church to the west, will be on the first floor, as well as the dining room. There will also be four reception rooms.

Construction started about a month ago, and the building is expected to be ready for occupancy by the middle of October. Ascension parish numbers about 1,300 families, and the present church was erected nearly ten years ago.

Chicago Daily News
July 8, 1939

Few realized, however, that Monsignor was in failing health and that his responsibilities and the difficulties of the depression and the war years were taking their toll. On Wednesday, March 29, 1944, Monsignor Cummings quietly passed away. Ascension's second pastor was dead.

His successor at Ascension, the Reverend Francis A. Ryan, wrote this tribute to him in the first issue of *The Dome*, the parish bulletin Father Ryan inaugurated:

> The first issue of "The Dome" is affectionately dedicated to the fond memory of our late beloved pastor Monsignor Cummings. Father Hanton and Father Keenan wish to join with the nuns and children of our school in asking all the parishioners to remember always the kindly Father whom God has called to his own ascension into Heaven. All will remember Monsignor for

The Ursulines at prayer in their new chapel.

his priestly bearing amongst us from the day of his coming until his untimely death. His presence here was only for a short span of time, yet he has built a monument in the hearts of his people that will stand forever. Monsignor Cummings was a princely gentleman, a man of prayer, a priest consumed with zeal for the cause of Charity. The Catholic Charities of the whole Archdiocese radiated life, and purpose, and achievement from his desk for more than twenty years. In the home of every needy family his name was synonymous with alleviation founded on the virtue so exalted by Christ Himself. The noble men of Saint Vincent De Paul brought a message of Hope to the afflicted as Monsignor Cummings sent them into every dark corner of our public institutions, hospitals, and homes for the aged. He was the Apostle of Charity, the Good Shepherd of the Poor. Thank God for the precious memory of him!

Remember Monsignor Cummings when you kneel in this beautiful Church of the Ascension. Pray for him. Remember Monsignor Cummings as he broke the Bread of Life for you, his children. Receive Holy Communion frequently for him. Every week for a whole year the Nuns will assist at the Holy Sacrifice of the Mass in the magnificent convent chapel that he erected for them. Your priests will always remember him at the Altar while you join with them to pray, "Grant, we beseech Thee, O Lord, that the soul of Thy servant, MONSIGNOR CUMMINGS, whom in this life Thou didst honor with the sacred office of the Holy Priesthood, may rejoice in the glory of Heaven for evermore, Amen." ✢

> *I was born in Ascension Parish in 1937. I have some fond memories of Ascension. . . . I remember the monthly movies, making First Communion as a class on Ascension Thursday, the Angels for the crib at Midnight Mass on Christmas Eve, the beautiful May Crownings. We also were treated to the circus each year, plus the end of the school year we went to the zoo for the lower grades and to Fullersburg Forest Preserves for a picnic for the higher grades.*
>
> ✢ *Marlene Manfredi Dreher*
> *Class of 1951*

CHAPTER THREE

Father Francis Ryan

1944–1951

Father Francis "Packy" Ryan was appointed Ascension's third pastor by Cardinal Samuel Stritch when Father Cummings died suddenly in 1944. In a way, Father Ryan was coming home. His family had moved to 531 S. Scoville Avenue, in Ascension Parish, shortly after his ordination. He had preached often at Ascension and had, at the request of his friend Father McDevitt, laid the cornerstone of the church.

Father Ryan was born August 8, 1898, one of eight children. He went to school at Old Saint Patrick's, Cathedral College (which later became Quigley Preparatory Seminary), and Saint Mary's Seminary in Baltimore, Maryland. Cardinal Mundelein ordained him at Holy Name Cathedral, December 17, 1921.

His first assignment was as the assistant to Bishop Edward F. Hoban, then auxiliary bishop of Chicago, and later bishop of the diocese of Cleveland. He served in this position for two years and developed a lifelong friendship with the bishop. He was the Vice-Chancellor of the archdiocese until 1929, when he opened Queen of All Saints in Sauganash. In 1934, Father Ryan became the pastor of Saint Leonard in Berwyn, where he remained until his assignment to Ascension.

The Dome

of the ASCENSION CHURCH — Oak Park, Illinois

REV. FRANCIS A. RYAN, *Pastor*

REV. A. W. HANTON } *Assistants*
REV. J. C. KEENAN

Rectory Phone { Euclid 40

Volume II — JANUARY 6, 1946 — The Epiphany — Number 36

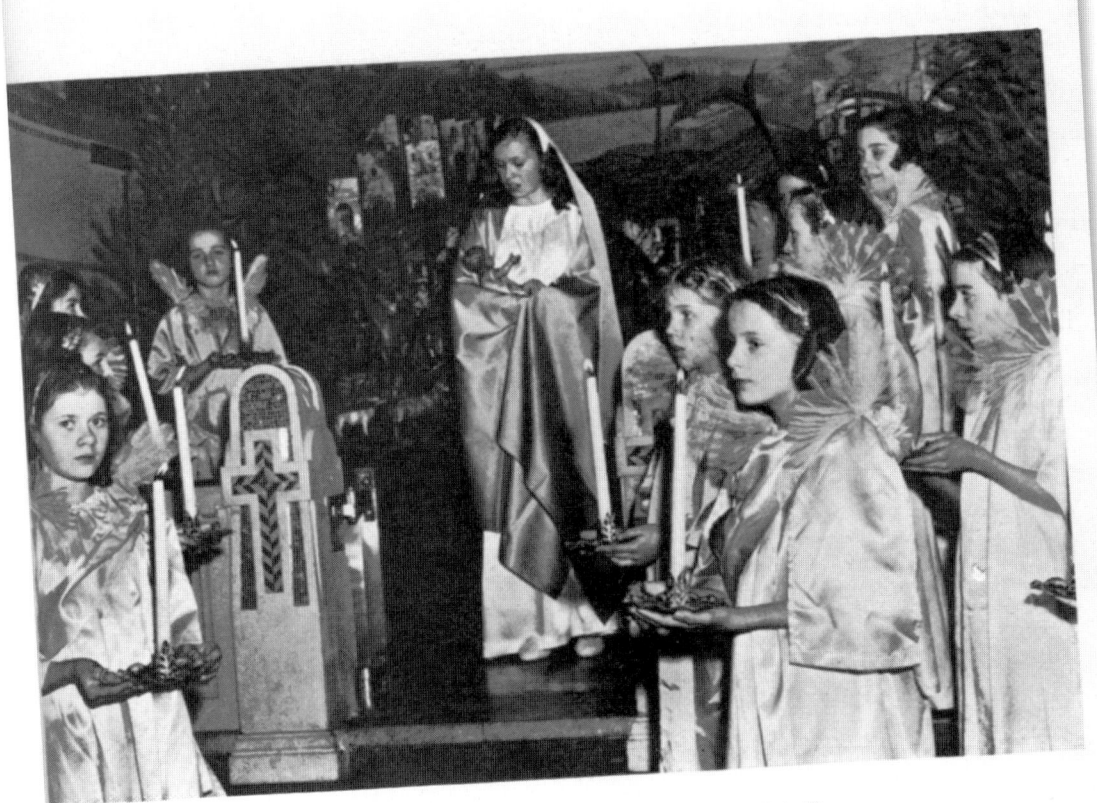

OUR CRIB *at* CHRISTMAS

A Legacy of Music

Father Ryan loved ceremony, and he loved beautiful things. He encouraged the development of an expanded musical presence at the liturgy, and very quickly Ascension gained a reputation for its music ministry. Ascension's Men and Boys Choir, directed by Alois Trnka, sang at High Masses but also performed in concert in Oak Park and throughout the Chicago area. Guest musicians, as many as a dozen at a time, came from the Chicago Symphony and the Chicago Opera Company. With the enthusiastic support of the pastor, the Pine Room Players produced plays each year. Mrs. Lorraine Thompson, the choir organist, also directed the school children in annual pageants. The students performed with their classmates, and all grade levels spent long hours in preparation for the big event each spring.

Father Ryan, seeking a way to inform, invite, and include his flock in parish life, began to write a weekly bulletin. *The Dome* was entirely his own project in the early years. He wrote it, typed it, and arranged for it to be published. Father Ryan's *Domes* are distinguished by their headlines (many with an exclamation point), their bowling scores, their lists of bingo winners, and their "Bless their hearts," his trademark expression.

The War Ends, New Growth Begins

The parish had helped with the United States war effort for four long years. Father Ryan wrote in *The Dome*:

> Mrs. Cassin, together with Mrs. Joseph Muriello, has been gathering food, cakes and cookies, for the Servicemen's Center for the past four years. Their splendid work is now completed. Mrs. Cassin writes this thanks to you—"During the past four

Chapter Three: Father Francis Ryan

Father Ryan officiates at a solemn High Mass.

years, the nuns, the parents, the pupils have cooperated perfectly in helping us to help the soldiers. We wish to thank every kind donor for every last cookie. The boys and girls in the service were so pleased when you thought so kindly of them. . . . They have now at last gone home, and so do we, thank you very, very much."

With the war ended, Ascension did what it could to help rebuild Europe. War Relief Services, an arm of the Bishops' Relief Campaign, collected food, money, and clothing for the aid of Europe, especially Poland, where the entire country had suffered tremendously during the German occupation. Children were asked to drop bundles of clothes at the back door of the rectory on their way to school. The Saint Vincent de Paul Society gathered the bundles and passed them on to the archdiocesan offices, which in turn shipped them overseas.

Father Ryan turned his energy to improving the facilities on the parish campus and preparing the school for the growth that would follow the war. An army of contractors

The Ursuline sisters, 1948–49.

The Ascension School football team, 1950.

and volunteers spent the summer of 1944 racing the clock to finish the work that had to be done before classes resumed in the fall.

On September 18 of that year, students returned to a "new" school. The cloakrooms had been removed and lockers installed in their stead; new fluorescent lighting illuminated the rooms, and new ceilings were insulated for sound. New desks, new flooring, and Venetian blinds for the windows made the classrooms very up-to-date. Father Ryan created the new Pine Room from the old parish hall and saw to it that it was in constant use. On October 15, with great fanfare, Cardinal Stritch blessed all the work that had been done. The children formed an honor guard while the Cardinal blessed the walls.

The cleaning-up energy did not stop in the school building; the church, too, although it was less than twenty years old, was given some of the finishing touches that it needed. The interior of the church received new carpets and drapes, additional lighting, a new candelabra, sanctuary lamps, and chimes. The work on the exterior included landscaping and additional lighting. A new flagpole, which was blessed at another ceremony in October, graced Van Buren Street.

> *Following World War II, after the Red Cross Unit disbanded, a group of ladies formed their own little sewing group to help St. Vincent's Orphanage. They sewed thousands of items of clothing and donated these and sums of money, raised by a party each year and other donations, to help those wonderful nuns and babies.*
>
> ✢ *Isabelle Vietzen*

Chapter Three: Father Francis Ryan

Ascension and World War Two

Father Ryan's *Dome* helped the parish keep track of its young men and women during the Second World War. Parishioners wrote to GIs and they wrote back, apprising the parish of their whereabouts, reassuring them of their safety. *The Dome* also announced the sad news of Ascension's thirty-two Gold-Star Mothers. These are some of the stories from *The Domes* of 1945. The headlines, and the exclamation points, are Father Ryan's, bless his heart!

Mrs. Grover Cox: Our Five Star Mother—*One Gold* and Four Blue!
. . . In every home of our parish God lent His graces to the hands and hearts of a ready and willing people. *"Mary, help our valiant soldiers"* was the battle hymn of our mothers and fathers. Mrs. Cox held back her tears so that her five children going off to war would learn their sublimest lesson of courage in the farewell smile of their mother. One daughter, Betty, was a member of the Waves; three sons, Captain Grover and Sergeant James of the Army; Lieutenant William of the Navy; and the youngest one of all—Private John J. Cox—will sleep forever in a hero's grave. . . .Bless the hearts of Cox's Army—what a great day in the morning for all our mothers and fathers when our boys come home. . . .

Our Gold Star Number Thirty-Two!
Mr. and Mrs. Michael De Rosa have received official word from the War Department of the death of their son, Sergeant Joseph M. De Rosa. Joseph was a crew member of a B-24 (Liberator) aircraft, which failed to return from a bombing mission to Linz, Austria. The aircraft developed mechanical difficulties and the crew was forced to bail out over the area around Kutina, Yugoslavia, into the Sava River. The notice of his death, which occurred December 15, 1944, was delayed this long in hopes that he would one day be found.

Happy Vacation for James L. Sender!
James LeRoy Sender, 901 S. Kenilworth Avenue, has been home on a twenty-one-day furlough. He is visiting with his mother, his brother Donald, and his grandmother, Mrs. Cora Collins. Jimmy has received his paratrooper's wings, called "the silver badge of courage," at Fort Benning, Georgia.

The Story of Private Edmund Brady!
Pfc. Edmund Brady, son of Mrs. Lillian Brady, graduated from Ascension School in 1936, from Fenwick in 1940. . . . As a rifleman, he fought through France and Germany for five months, until, while on a patrol with four other men, he was surrounded by SS troops. Wounded in the foot, he was forced to surrender. He and ninety other prisoners were herded into one boxcar and for three days rode across Germany with no food or water. After remaining in a prison camp for several weeks, he was shipped to a bombed city where he was put to work removing [the] dead, and clearing bombed-out buildings. The prisoners lived as best they could, stealing food and clothing whenever possible. To keep the prisoners out of the path of advancing Americans, the Germans marched the prisoners deeper into Germany. Seeing an excellent chance to escape, Ed and five others escaped into the woods. . . . Ed is now on a sixty-day furlough, and then will go to Florida to an army rest camp. . . .

The Navolio Boys!
Sergeant Charlie Robert Navolio has been stationed in England for three years. He was with the 305th Bombers, 8th Air Force. Charles is on his way home. Bob was a waist gunner during the terrific days of the battle of Buttan. And did this Bob distinguish himself—he won Miss Joyce Linehan, of Somerset, England as a bride for prize number one. He merited the Air Medal, the Distinguished Flying Cross, the Good Conduct Medal, the Presidential Unit Citation, and Six Oak Leaf Clusters. Lieutenant John Jr. is located in Harlingen, Texas. He has just completed a course in overseas training.

Corporal Dennis J. Crowley Serves His Country!

. . . Dennis arrived in England, December 13, 1943, and was assigned to the 9th Infantry Division of the First Army. He was right in there pitching on D-Day, and the crossing of the English Channel, says the boy, "was something I shall never forget to my dying day." Dennis was awarded the Silver Star, . . . was wounded in the Hurtgen Forest, . . . and wears the campaign ribbons of five major engagements. At present he is looking the situation over in a small town near Munich.

Sergeant Dixie Carraher, Bless His Heart!

". . . It's just a little over a year ago that Father Keenan took all of us on a lake cruise; this time I was on one of Uncle Sam's ships headed for the Philippines. While in Manila I was connected with a unit of entertainers, and I performed in a show called "Fall Out for Fun." My job in the army is with the Special Service Office, which takes care of all entertainment, athletics, and recreation for the men. We performed at nine hospitals in Manila and were well received at all of them. Performing for men who have been in many hard battles and who are wounded severely is something I will never forget. . . . I am now working with the Far Eastern Air Service Command Special Services. I just had a pleasant visit with Corporal Tom Gavin from our parish and the Chaplain of our outfit is a Chicago priest, Father Robert Henely. My best wishes to all at home, signed, Dixie Carraher."

The Padre of the Purple Heart

My dear Father Ryan,

Greetings to all my friends at Ascension from the "Padre of the Purple Heart." By this time, you must have read in all the daily papers that I was wounded. I am now a hero, though as modest and as approachable as ever. Here is my story. It happened one night about nine o'clock. I was awakened out of a sound sleep by the firing of ack-ack guns. It usually takes a cannon or two to wake me up. As is my custom on such occasions, I leaped from the sack, grabbed my helmet and slippers, put them on in order, and hastily beat a path for the bomb shelter. No sooner had I entered when I heard an enemy plane, seemingly directly overhead. The inevitable crash came in the form of a 120–200 pound "daisy-cutter"—an anti-personnel bomb. The blooming thing landed only fifteen feet from the entrance to the shelter. A flying piece of shrapnel hit me in

Captain John F. Loftus, Army Chaplain.

the leg. As a result I have been here in the hospital for the past three weeks. . . . All goes well, despite the efforts of the enemy to make this place uncomfortable. The soldiers respond real earnestly, and I am happy to tell you that we have a well-organized Holy Name Society. That's a great deal out here, where the men may at times be inclined to use strong language. . . . Ask my friends to write to me. I wish to join the others in sending you fifty cents for Angelo.

With kindest regards to all, yours in the Purple Heart,
Father John F. Loftus

(Father Loftus was an associate at Ascension from 1937 to 1943 and a favorite among the young people of the parish.)

The Ascension Holy Name Society Bowling League, 1946–47.

The Women's Bowling League.

Father Ryan's Bowling Report

✠

Joe Radke Hit a 589!

Read the above score, and tell your grandchildren about it. It set a track record for the new bowlers club. One man, strongman Joe Radke, hit 589!...A new high was set by Catherine Scharf, who rolled a 497, think of it, wonderful, terrific! Bernice Anderson was chasing her plenty with a 477; Mary Martin, 444; and Helen Johnson, 316....The first place honors are the crown and glory of Father Ryan's Holy Rollers, 33–18. Shovelling into second place are the Coalmen of O'Keefes, 32–19. Eating their heads off in third place are the Del Marre Beaners. Pumping gas in fourth place are the Herb Rentner Gassers. The light of fifth place is gleaming from Hansen Candle Bearers. The clean glass of sixth place is the work of Andy's Servicemen. The fire and theft policy for last place is guaranteed by the Ed Riley Underwriters....Joe Radke throws that ball around like a ping-pong, like a feather, like a demon. His score last week was 686....At last it can be told. Johnny Kallal tells the world his story. His future, his ambitions, his success—it's bowling! Nothing else matters with John because he is now King Pin Bowler—last week with a score of 761! Forever John will be content to live in the Alleys when he can roll such a magnificent average!...Johnny go-to-market so went three times over the Ray McGraths. The Drugs of Johnson eclipsed the little Pastorettes twice. The Lady Embalmers did that twice for the Marge Crowleys. The Stobarts lulled a twin sleep over the Wallace Kandy Kids.... Set 'em up boys and here's the way they knock 'em down: C. Campbell, 232; J. Cagney, 200....Johnny Kallal fixed a fire engine and rode it right down the alley last Wednesday. Hercules Kallal hit a 202, a 203, a 223, and finished up in a five-eleven blaze of glory—628 for Kallal. When the smoke cleared, his team of Carry-Outers had burnt the Hansen Candles to a mere sputter.

Excerpts from Fr. Ryan's reports of the parish bowling league scores
The Dome, 1947

The cost for all this work and for some improvements made to the convent and the rectory totaled $132,770. It was paid by parishioners between 1944 and October 1946 through a parish "subscription," a two-week drive early in September each year during which parishioners pledged their support. The subscriptions of 1945 and 1946 paid for the most recent work in full. Father Ryan announced that the only parish debt was the $60,000 still owed to the Archdiocese for the construction loan for the convent. Father Ryan was ebullient in his gratitude: "This is your record! You have done all things well! You are to be highly congratulated! You rightfully deserve our sincerest thanks! God bless you abundantly for the treasure you have stored up for His Home on Earth! God keep you forever in His loving care! Bless your hearts always!"

Chapter Three: Father Francis Ryan

Baseball team, date unknown.

In July of 1946, the statue of Mary, Queen of Peace, was erected on the rectory lawn. It was the gift of John and Cecelia Brennan in memory of their son John Thomas, a member of the class of 1934. He was killed in action in January 1945 and was buried in France.

Angelo Marcrino, the caretaker for whose benefit Father Ryan would always ask "and fifty cents for Angelo," shared Father Ryan's predilection for a beautiful campus. With the new landscaping and the illumination of the statue of Mary, Angelo suggested to Father Ryan, who quoted him in *The Dome*, "Father should no say, fifty cents for Angelo. Now Father should say one dollar!"

Ascension opened its first kindergarten classroom in the basement of the five-year-old convent in 1944.

> *"Give fifty cents for Angelo." Every Sunday, Father Ryan would remind us in the Dome that Angelo needed the money. We found out that Angelo was a gardener who worked for the Chicago Park District. Spring arrived, and the landscaping around the church and rectory was beautiful. Flowers bloomed from spring to late fall. Father Ryan had "connections," and one of them was Angelo!*
>
> ☩ *Lou Frillman*

Ascension's first kindergarten class, 1945.

Armistice Day activities at Ascension.

War bond sales, 1946.

Chapter Three: Father Francis Ryan

The School Mural

In the summer of 1998, Ascension School underwent a major renovation. The entire interior of the first floor of the building was stripped down to a shell, and it was all put back together sounder, safer, brighter, and more attractive than it had been. In that stripping down, wallpaper that had covered the walls of the Pine Room lobby was removed and, to the amazement of the workers, a mural was revealed.

The work proceeded with much more caution when it became clear that the mural was in good shape. Tim Lennon, an expert conservator, examined the painting at the request of the Ascension community. In a letter dated October 26, 1998, Mr. Lennon wrote:

> The mural is an oil on plaster (there is no intermediate canvas layer on the wall) measuring approximately H. 8 feet x W. 12 feet, the overall shape being a rectangle with a curved bottom edge. The painting is signed in the lower right corner M. Gaspar and dated 1944. This identifies the artist Miklos Gaspar, 1885–1946, a noted regional painter whose murals decorate a number of public and private institutions around the Midwest.... Gaspar was an artist of sound training and great experience, and the materials and techniques used in the creation of this mural were all first rate. ...This mural may well have been the artist's last work.

Further research revealed more about the artist and his career. Miklos Gaspar was born in Budapest, Hungary, and served as the official war artist for the Austro-Hungarian government during World War I. He immigrated to Chicago in 1921. His murals cover the walls of prominent buildings in the Midwest, including a room at Chicago's Union League Club. Gaspar painted forty murals for the General Motors building for the 1933 World's Fair. When the fair closed, the murals were transported to Lane Tech High School in Chicago, making the school, in the words of Flora Doody, the art restoration director at Lane, "a mini-museum."

The mural depicts a priest and a nun, each leading a group of children toward the figure of a teaching Jesus in the center. The children wear clothes of different eras; the priest is thought to represent Ascension's second pastor, Monsignor Cummings, and the nun, Mother Victorine. It was painted in 1944 as part of the work that created the Pine Room of the parish hall and presumably was commissioned by Father Ryan.

No one is quite certain why the mural was covered, or when. People who were students in the 1960s seem to disagree whether or not the picture was visible when they were there. Mr. Lennon surmises: "I can easily imagine that the painting, a very contemporary image at the time of its creation, fell out of fashion a decade or two afterward and was covered over in a well-intentioned redecorating scheme. Now more than a half century after the creation of the painting, it takes on a nostalgic quality evoking a simpler time of patriotic and religious belief.... Briefly, it is a very good painting, and the parish should be very pleased with its recovery."

It was determined that the painting needed very little conservation treatment. The unfortunate placement of an electrical outlet in the center of the picture, at Jesus' knee, suggested to some that work should be done to remove it, but more damage likely would have occurred in the process. At any rate, the mural today again bids its viewers: "Suffer children to come to me, and forbid them not, for of such is the kingdom of heaven" (Luke 18:16).

(The classroom would move in 1951 to the old Spinner home on Clarence Avenue, where it would remain until 1958.) During Father Ryan's administration, the 9:00 Mass on Sunday was for children only—and all children were expected to attend. They gathered in school at 8:50 and processed into church; they needed a note from home if they were found to have missed Mass. Classes started daily at 8:50; children were encouraged to attend daily Mass at 8:15, but it was not required. Father Ryan wrote that it was "highly recommended that they pay a visit to the Blessed Sacrament on their way to school."

Five hundred and ninety-four children were enrolled in Ascension School in 1946; that number would double in the next

> *Ascension Parish means Home. One of my sons said, "It's the same thing you can count on." Wow! That is so true. I have been an Ascensionite since 1948. I wasn't too active in the parish then. When I taught school here and then was married here in 1959, that's when it really began. The people are still my friends.*
>
> ☦ *Mary Jean (Walsh) Connelly*

Second-grade classroom, 1950. Classes continued to grow until 1966.

Chapter Three: Father Francis Ryan

> *Do, Re, Mi—Father Ryan used to sing this ditty to us:*
>
> *"BINGO on Friday, bless your hearts,
> Come to the Pine Room, that's where it starts."*
>
> ✣ *Sally Latus*

fifteen years as soldiers came home from the war and began their families. Alois Trnka recruited the returning soldiers for the choir, Father Ryan recruited them for the bowling league, and the Knights of Columbus recruited them to join their group, which still met at 641 S. Scoville, Ascension's first property. New members were called the Ryan Jubilee Class, in honor of Father Ryan's twenty-fifth anniversary in the priesthood.

When the 1950–1951 school year began, more than 725 children registered for classes. Father Ryan requested that plans be drawn for an addition to the building. These plans included classrooms, a gymnasium, and a place for the youth of the parish to gather; such additions would be made in later years, but according to a different set of plans.

Bless His Heart

Father Ryan was a very popular pastor. One student remembered his visits to the classroom as "Santa Claus without the costume; when he'd be ready to leave the room, suddenly quarters would fall all over the floor." He was charming and warm-hearted; his door was always open. His energy was essential to the work of building a new community at the war's end, and he spent it unstintingly for Ascension and south Oak Park.

His sudden death on January 10, 1951, stunned the parish. Many parish families had been part of Ascension for several decades; many of them had experienced the unexpected death of each of the three pastors. They had lost another leader and friend. ✢

The statue of Mary, Queen of Peace, lovingly tended by Joe Massura.

A Tribute to Father Ryan

✠

The beloved pastor of Ascension entered into his eternal reward Wednesday, January 10, 1951, in the 52nd year of his life and the 29th year of his priesthood. May his soul and the souls of all the faithful departed through the mercy of God rest in peace.

Father Ryan's death came suddenly, unexpectedly, in the quiet hours just before dawn. Apparently fully recovered from a recent period of serious illness, he had retired Tuesday evening in good spirits and with no apparent warning of the forthcoming summons of his Maker.

Father Ryan's gifts were uncountable. Few men in or out of religion could approach his oratory. Words—beautiful, consoling, soul-inspiring—fell from his lips in a seemingly effortless pattern. His personal charm was infectious and lovable. He had a flair for pageantry, surrounding our church, our altars, our music with a beauty that became famous archdiocese-wide, if not nationwide. His wit and repartee were most refreshing. He had a natural love of children and showered upon them untold pleasures and gifts. He believed the House of God should be immaculate and beautiful.

"Bless your heart," wrote Father Ryan in the very first issue of *The Dome*. This became more and more his trademark, as it was his creed. When on occasion it was said to him he acknowledged it graciously, as he did in 1945 when he wrote in *The Dome*:

> "Bless your heart" was said to me
> In such a kindly way
> How often I remember it
> This phrase from yesterday.
> Three simple words that's all and yet
> What tender warmth they had
> And he who spoke them never knew
> Those words had made me glad.
> I often wish a phrase of mine
> Could cheer somebody's day
> As "bless your heart" was said to me
> In such a kindly way.

Above all, Father Ryan was a priest, a true disciple of Christ the High Priest. He knew the inestimable dignity of the Mass, his Mass, where with hands consecrated to God he brought the Crucified Savior daily to our altar. He knew and exercised his power to forgive our sins in Christ's name. He brought the light of salvation to our children in Baptism. He united our young men and women in the Holy Sacrament of Matrimony. He comforted our dying with Extreme Unction. He pronounced the last words of absolution when our loved ones were taken from us, as he has now been. In all of his priestly duties he was the true follower of Christ, recognizing the dignity and sanctity of his high calling and willingly assuming the burdens as well as the grace it brought.

We of Ascension have lost our pastor. We have lost a friend. . . . We will miss him. But we will never forget him, what he did for us, for our church, for God.

Excerpted from *The Dome*, January 14, 1951
Written by a parishioner

CHAPTER FOUR

Monsignor John D. Fitzgerald

1951–1973

Upon the death of Father Ryan, Cardinal Stritch appointed his own private secretary, the Very Reverend John D. Fitzgerald, as pastor of Ascension. Monsignor Fitzgerald was a learned man with a doctorate in Canon Law from the Gregorian University in Rome. He had a great flair for writing, and his regular column in the Dome, "A Word with You," was a beautifully composed reflection on life and parish activities.

Illustrative of Monsignor Fitzgerald's local and national stature is the fact that it was Ascension's rectory that was chosen in 1952 for a private meeting between President Truman and Cardinal Stritch. The President's visit was secret, with no advance notice to the press, the parishioners, or the neighbors. The President was concerned about the coming presidential election and wanted to consult with the Cardinal regarding the Catholic vote for Adlai Stevenson, his presumptive heir.

The Ascension generation that was ushered in with the death of Father Ryan and the arrival of Monsignor Fitzgerald as pastor was extraordinary for its enormous growth, not only in sheer numbers of parishioners but also in rising to meet unprecedented changes in the Church and society. From the relative calm and insular life of the 1950s through the upheaval in the Church and social institutions that marked the 1960s and early 1970s, Ascension walked a new path, balancing respect for a rich tradition with response to a changing reality—all within a context of fidelity to Christ's teaching.

of the ASCENSION CHURCH • Oak Park, Illinois

RT. REV. MSGR. JOHN D. FITZGERALD, Pastor

Assistants
REV. THOMAS W. RIORDAN - REV. JOHN J. POWERS - REV. BERNARD C. WHITE

Rectory Phone
VIllage 8-2703

VOLUME XX   November 10, 1963 — Twenty-third Sunday after Pentecost   No. 11

PANTRY SHOWER and CARD PARTY

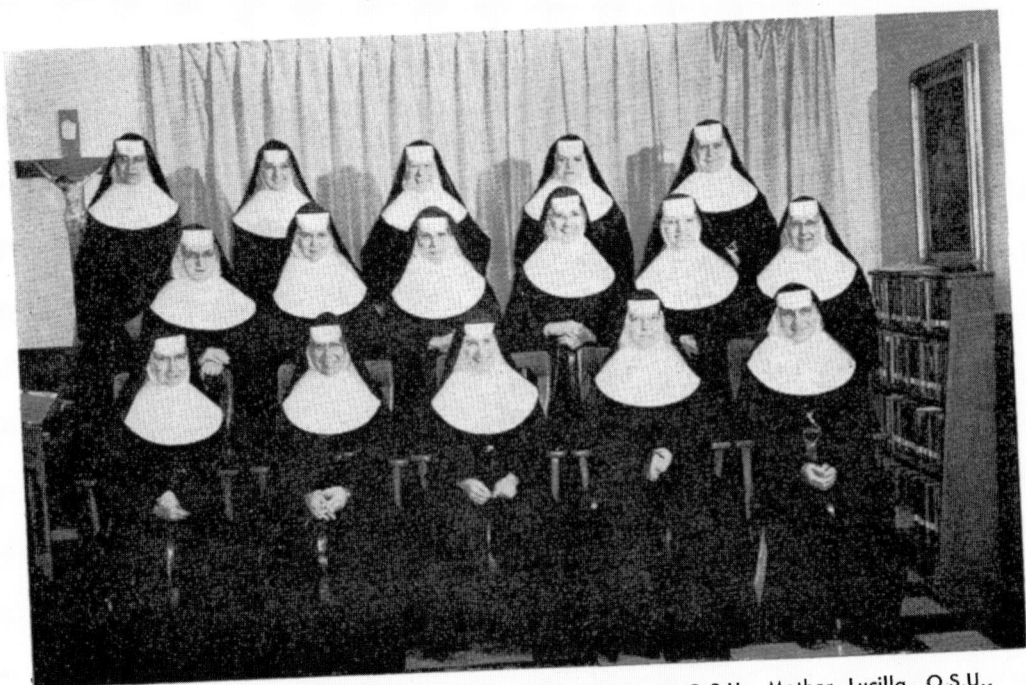

Seated, first row: Mother Cordula, O.S.U., Mother Theodore, O.S.U., Mother Lucilla, O.S.U., Mother Edna, O.S.U., Mother Charlotte, O.S.U.

Second row: Mother Columba, O.S.U., Mother Beatrice, O.S.U., Mother Angela, O.S.U., Mother Lois, O.S.U., Mother Gabriel, O.S.U., Mother Frances Clare, O.S.U.

Top row: Mother James Marie, O.S.U., Mother Mary John, O.S.U., Mother Catherine, O.S.U., Mother Imelda, O.S.U., Mother Thomas, O.S.U.

The end of the Second World War saw the return of soldiers to their families and a newfound relative affluence, due in part to the ability to finance college educations on the GI Bill. Many families were launched into an unanticipated middle or upper-middle class existence. Homeownership and suburban life became a reality, and families grew in number to fill the homes that were purchased in south Oak Park. The area south of Jackson Boulevard between Ridgeland and Oak Park Avenue became known as "the Fertile Crescent," as many families of ten or twelve children filled the frame homes. In 1960, 267 baptisms were performed at Ascension—an average of twenty-two new babies a month!

Parish Community Life in the 1950s

The sheer numbers of parishioners, fueled by the postwar prosperity and the large families in the parish, necessitated an addition to the school that included a gym, youth center, kindergarten, and more classrooms. The new facilities were dedicated in October 1954, and the youth center was named in honor of Father Ryan.

Such facilities were necessary because the parish was the center of social life for most parishioners. Catholics were viewed with suspicion, especially in 1950s Oak Park, which was overwhelmingly Republican, mainline Protestant, and white. Many social organizations did not allow Catholics as members. Some broader social acceptance and understanding of Catholics on a societal level had begun as a result of the immense popularity of 1940s Hollywood films such as *Going My Way* and *The Keys of the Kingdom*. The use of Latin in the Mass and other traditional religious practices, however, were not understood by the larger society, and

Cardinal Stritch blessed the addition to Ascension School in 1954.

Chapter Four: Monsignor John D. Fitzgerald

hence perceived as foreign and strange. As a result, for the successive waves of immigrant Catholics that had come from all over Europe and Latin America in the nineteenth and early twentieth centuries, parishes became virtually self-contained urban social structures. Ascension was typical in its social offerings, which included men's and women's bowling leagues, boxing teams, roller skating in the gym after school and on weekends, and "canteen"—a soda fountain–style establishment with windows that overlooked the gym. The emphasis on sports was similar to the operations of the YMCA (an organization that Catholics were discouraged from joining) and was designed to strengthen families by encouraging men to be involved in parish activities.

Various gender-based parish organizations promoted the spiritual mission of the Church and helped foster community within the parish. High school girls were encouraged to join the Sodality of Our Lady of Fatima for prayer and social activities. In a January 1960 *Dome*, Monsignor Fitzgerald invited the young Sodality women to 8:00 a.m. Mass on Saturday morning and to remain afterward to pray for "peace and reparation." The Sodality also sponsored an annual May Crowning to honor the Blessed Mother. In addition to continuing what Father McDevitt once described as the "backbone" work of the parish, the Altar and Rosary Society met monthly for Mass and recitation of the Rosary, and sponsored social events such as card parties and fashion shows. Bunco and canasta games were regular events for seniors, while young mothers ran the annual "Cookie Walk."

> *My favorite memory was the day I married Tom Slott. The Ursulines were still semi-cloistered then, so were unable to attend our wedding Mass, officiated by Msgr. Fitzgerald. Since they couldn't come to the reception, we had a catered meal delivered to the convent. The nuns insisted I go to the convent right after Mass. Reminds me of The Sound of Music. They checked everything out—the veil, the gown, the petticoat, etc. I was surrounded. Everyone was laughing and talking at once. Then they did something else so unexpected; they gave us a gift—a lovely crucifix. How loving! We were told to take it on our honeymoon, and to kneel down to pray with each of us holding a hand over an arm of Jesus. We did as instructed. That was September 1, 1951. Next September 1st will be our 56th wedding anniversary. The crucifix is still on our bedroom wall. So you see, the Ursulines and Ascension memories are still and will always be with us.*
>
> ✝ *Norine Kresich Slott*

School Library Board, 1957.

The Holy Name Society organized dances, father-daughter Communion breakfasts, and Sports Nights. This men's group maintained a list of street captains charged with visiting Catholic homes and inviting the men in the house to join the organization. Minutes from a Holy Name Society meeting on September 19, 1955, sheds light on other ministries of the group. The Sick and Vigil Committee provided social support, such as visiting ill members and attending the wakes of the deceased. Members were encouraged to attend the Holy Hour on Friday evenings. Envelopes collected on Holy Name Communion Sundays were recorded and attendance numbers closely monitored as to how many members were receiving Communion. The Literature Committee checked local newsstands and business establishments for "salacious literature," encouraged higher quality TV programs, sponsored a parish library, and promoted radio programs such as Monsignor Fulton Sheen's broadcasts on WMAQ. Notes from the same 1955 meeting include a report from member Frank Gheselli, who shared a list of local

> *In 1954, we came to Ascension as newlyweds. All five of our children graduated from Ascension School. Three of the five were married here. Two of our twelve grandchildren were baptized here. Ascension Parish has formed and influenced our family structure, memories, faith, and accomplishments.*
>
> ☩ *Pat and Bill McNichols*

Chapter Four: Monsignor John D. Fitzgerald

stores and barbershops found with inappropriate literature. It was decided to mail these merchants letters of concern, "after which time personal calls will be made on them."

More corporal works of mercy were undertaken by organizations such as Our Lady's Volunteers, whose members baked cookies for shut-ins and assisted the aged, the infirm, bereaved families, and young families in need of help. The St. Vincent de Paul Society assisted parishioners in financial need. The Medical Mission Society collected "bandages, baby blankets, bedsheets, [and other items] badly needed for the mission field," according to the *Dome* of October 9, 1960. Ascension's chapter of the Knights of Columbus afforded an opportunity for men to provide service and to support the parish and the local community, and, as part of a national organization, promote Catholic education and influence government policies.

The twins at Ascension School made the news in 1959.

Kathy Pinter, George Holly, and Mary Jane Joyce (class of '69) join Monsignor Fitzgerald in welcoming Mother Felicia, OSU, Mother General of the Ursuline Sisters, to Ascension. With Monsignor are Mother Lois and Mother Lucilla.

    As much as Ascension could be considered a social community unto itself, it was still very much integrated into the larger community of Oak Park and the rapidly growing Archdiocese of Chicago. In the 1950s, Oak Park was the center of local commerce and entertainment, and parishioners enjoyed shopping at stores such as Gilmore's and dining at nearby Nielsen's and Horwath's. Plans were made to construct a modern east-west highway that would connect Oak Park with downtown and the emerging western suburbs. That meant, however, that a geographic slice would be made through the parish, and the

Chapter Four: Monsignor John D. Fitzgerald

Room 206, 1959.

Ascension School Faculty, 1958–1959.

60   Ascension Centennial 1907–2007

proposed highway exit at East Avenue would bring more traffic and congestion near the Church and school. Monsignor Fitzgerald wrote about his concern in the weekly *Dome*:

> Since the Congress Street highway begins to assume form more tangible than dim hope backdropping a terrifying traffic nightmare, it behooves us to think.... We appear to be faced with a controllable future reality. To eventuate happily, we will have to nudge it our way according to plan.

Monsignor Fitzgerald's influence was so great that he succeeded in having the plans for an East Avenue exit from the Congress Expressway (to be renamed the Eisenhower) scrapped. Apparently, he was a good friend of Senator Everett McKinley Dirksen, who ultimately was responsible for the decision not to build the exit. The incident is mentioned in an article, "The Neglected Political Economy of Eminent Domain" by Nicole Stelle Garnett in the October 2006 *Michigan Law Review*:

> Two bends in the [Eisenhower] were made at the behest of Monsignor William Gorman of Resurrection parish, who also objected to plans to divide his parish, and Monsignor John D. Fitzgerald of Ascension parish, who killed plans for an off-ramp into his parish. Perhaps not surprisingly ... these men served on the Archdiocese's steering committee for "neighborhood conservation."

> *Joe and I were married here in 1953. So we know something about and love all the people who make the Sunday liturgy and parish so beautiful. Inspiration and support comes from those who are part of "Extending the Word" small faith community, too.*
>
> *It's my family with whom I find inspiration and opportunity to serve. I am 81 years old, so know many parishioners and am encouraged by their example. What a boost Christmas morning offered even though our fine choirs had sung Christmas Eve. David on the organ accompanied by a joyful trumpet was great! Who decorated the beautiful sanctuary and manger scenes? The fine visiting priests offer challenging and comforting words.*
>
> ☩ *Mary Massura*

Parish Spiritual Life

Monsignor Fitzgerald's intervention kept the corner of East Avenue and Van Buren safe for pedestrian traffic—much needed for parishioners making their way to one of seven Masses offered on Sundays, five on weekdays, and nine on Holy Days of Obligation.

There were no evening Masses allowed, so to accommodate the parish faithful, Masses were scheduled approximately every hour on the hour from 6:00 a.m. to 12:15 p.m. on Sundays and every half hour from 6:30 a.m. to 8:45 a.m. on weekdays. Three assistant priests and one resident priest helped Monsignor Fitzgerald with the exhaustive Mass schedule. The Tridentine Mass was conducted in Latin with only the Scripture readings and sermon in English. Masses were designated as either "High Mass" (a more ritualized service in which the priest was often accompanied by a deacon [or another priest serving as deacon] and portions of the Mass were chanted rather than recited) or "Low Mass" (a shorter, simpler service in which the priest recites the prayers). There was usually only one High Mass per week, and more time was allotted for that Mass on the schedule. The faithful in the pews either prayed quietly or followed along with their missals, with the "Ordinary of the Mass" printed in Latin on one side and the English translation on the facing page.

Cardinal Stritch leaves Ascension Church to bless the school addition, 1954.

The spiritual life of Ascensionites was also fed with frequent Communion, but the regulations before receiving were strict. In the early 1950s, healthy communicants had to fast from food and drink beginning at midnight the night before. A 1954 *Dome* article provided an update that the "drinking of plain water no longer breaks the Eucharistic fast." The report also outlines provisions for the sick, those "performing exhausting labor," and the faithful traveling a considerable distance to church as being allowed to take liquid nourishment up to one hour before receiving Communion.

Community prayer took the form of regular novenas and popular devotions such as Forty Hours and the Holy Hour. The Apostleship of Prayer connected the parishioners with the intentions of the Holy Father and the universal church. Both the Holy Name Society and

All of Ascension School celebrated Monsignor Fitzgerald's anniversary.

Altar and Rosary sponsored annual retreats. Parishioner Fred Hanson organized and led many retreats for men on a parish and diocesan level. In recognition of his service to the Church, the Papal order of Knighthood of St. Sylvester was conferred upon Fred in 1957 by Cardinal Stritch on behalf of Pope Pius XII.

Formation in the faith was conducted in various manners. Children attending the parish school were under the tutelage of the Ursuline Sisters. Public-grade-school children attended CCD classes, and teens not enrolled in Catholic high schools were required to attend the Tuesday evening Chi-Ro Club. The Holy Name and Altar and Rosary societies had speakers at their monthly meetings. The Inquiry Club was a weekly hour-long presentation by one of the parish priests and was open to anyone, Catholic or not, who wanted to know more about the various facets of the Catholic faith. A March 1954 *Dome* article advertises an upcoming presentation:

Chapter Four: Monsignor John D. Fitzgerald

Cussin' and swearin' will be discussed (but not demonstrated) by Father Shields at the Inquiry Class tomorrow evening when he treats the second and subsequent commandments.

The late 1950s saw the beginning of the Christian Family Movement at Ascension. Begun as a lay movement fifteen years earlier in Chicago, the Christian Family Movement was a national network of prayer and reflection groups sponsored by parishes but based in neighborhoods. Members met regularly in each other's homes and reflected upon Scripture in light of what was occurring in their personal and community lives. Christian values were reinforced, and families were encouraged both to grow in faith and to be involved in their community. The network, leadership, and commitment of the "CFMers" at Ascension contributed to the parish's leading role in the tumult and upheaval that characterized Oak Park in the 1960s.

Church Life in the 1960s

Many of the parish devotions and organizations continued to feed the spiritual and community needs of Ascensionites as the parish entered the 1960s. The baby boom of the 1950s saw the parish school reach a peak attendance of twelve hundred students in 1964. There were up to three classes for each grade. Community-building activities, such as the Holy Name Society's steak fries, roller-skating in the gym, and Altar and Rosary fashion shows, continued. However, the winds of change were beginning to blow in the institutional Church, Oak Park, and the nation. The parish community, already highly organized and led very capably by Monsignor Fitzgerald, faced these changes head-on, making Ascension one of the most vibrant and influential parishes in the archdiocese.

It is commonly felt that the College of Cardinals elected Cardinal Angelo Roncalli pope in 1958 with the idea that his ministry would be short and uneventful because of his advanced age

[In the 1950s, I] attended first, second, third, [and] fourth grades and then moved to California. When I started there, I was a grade ahead because of my great education at Ascension. I remember going to class in second grade in the attic of the convent across the street because of overcrowding! The kindergarten had a small stove, refrigerator, and great wooden utensils. There was a reading room that was quite beautiful! We called the sisters "Mother."

✢ *Joan Kevil Engel Montague*

The Distinguished Visitor

✠

On a grey Saturday afternoon in November of 1951, I parked my car in front of the rectory before going to Confession in church. No sooner was I parked than a black limousine drove up in back of my car, and a young man in a black overcoat alighted and came over and asked me would I mind moving my car.

My natural curiosity got the better of me and I said, "Why?"—whereupon he politely informed me that "a distinguished person" was coming to pay a visit to our Ascension Rectory, and they wanted to park directly in front. So, I moved my car about 150 feet south, approximately in front of what was then the Kay Moore house.

I immediately turned off the engine and walked back toward the rectory only to see another limousine drive up, with four Secret Service men getting out and starting to escort a rather short, dapper, grey-overcoated man up the sidewalk into the priest's house.

I said to the Secret Service man whom I was standing close to by that time, that the visitor looked like "Mr. Truman." He turned to me with a big grin—and promptly said, "It is!" Mr. Truman had come to see Cardinal Stritch, who was then visiting our own Monsignor Fitzgerald in Ascension Rectory!

Needless to say—I don't recall going to Confession that day—but I DO vividly remember how thrilling it was seeing the 33rd President of the United States, Harry S. Truman, "a distinguished visitor" going into Ascension Rectory that Saturday afternoon in November!

Helen M. Craig
Class of '27
From Fiftieth Anniversary Book

and precarious health. Yet as Pope John XXIII, he called for a Second Vatican Council to renew the Church and "throw open its windows," brought about radical changes in the Church and religious life that came home to Ascension in sometimes painful, other times liberating, ways. The Tridentine Mass was replaced by the "New Mass" with prayers spoken in English rather than the traditional Latin. The altar was turned around (or in many cases a new altar was installed) so that the priest faced the congregation rather than standing turned away from them. The altar rails were removed, and reception of Holy Communion under both species was encouraged. Monsignor Fitzgerald made provisional changes to the interior of the church in response to the mandates of the Second Vatican Council before he initiated more radical remodeling in 1971.

> *When Cardinal Stritch died [in 1958], kids got out of school to line Jackson Boulevard for the cemetery procession.*
>
> ☩ *Bill Winters*

As in the church everywhere, Mass in the vernacular ("the language of the people") sometimes meant the music of the people, too. Guitar masses appealed to young people and to families whose teens found the relevance of the music attractive. Ascension started a Sunday Mass in the gym, a relaxed and intimate gathering that led to the formation of many strong friendships and formed many people for ministry. The "Gym Mass" began to allow for more lay leadership and liturgical innovation. The emergence of lay leadership helped fill the void as many priests and nuns left their congregations to pursue different roles and ministries.

Ascension Parish continued to be a source of spiritual nourishment and guidance during the tumult and transition that affected not only Oak Park and its neighboring communities but also the nation itself in the late 1960s and early 1970s. A decade that saw

The banquet in the gym followed the dedication of the new school building, 1954.

the assassination of major political leaders, the civil rights movement, race rioting, women's liberation struggles, discontent with the Church's teachings on matters of family life, and other upheavals resulted in a loss of confidence in societal institutions. At Ascension, Monsignor Fitzgerald aligned himself and the parish with civic movements that advanced Oak Park and its residents, both Catholic and non-Catholic. Ascension's leadership was especially active in the creation of Oak Park's Fair Housing Act.

The riots that tore apart the West Side of Chicago following the assassination of the Reverend Dr. Martin Luther King, Jr., in April 1968 keenly affected Oak Park as well. Although the fires never crossed Austin Boulevard, many families were afraid their homes were at peril and were ready to flee farther west at a moment's notice. When the rioting ended, many families on the West Side had lost everything. Ascensionites joined other Oak Parkers in collecting food, clothing, furniture, bedding, and other household supplies for the devastated families. Some Oak Parkers welcomed affected families into their homes until more permanent housing could be arranged. More challenging than the immediate needs of the families, however, was the direction Oak Park would take as a community in response to racial tensions and the growing civil rights movement.

The riots and "white flight" that affected Chicago's Austin neighborhood just east of Oak Park had the parish and larger community in fear that their neighborhoods would witness the same block-by-block "turnover" fed by blockbusting and panic peddling. Monsignor Fitzgerald responded by working with village leaders and organizing community meetings in the Pine Room that were often acrimonious and emotional. One side was concerned with fairness, justice, and what they saw as the Gospel response to the times; the other side argued their fears for their homes, families, and way of life.

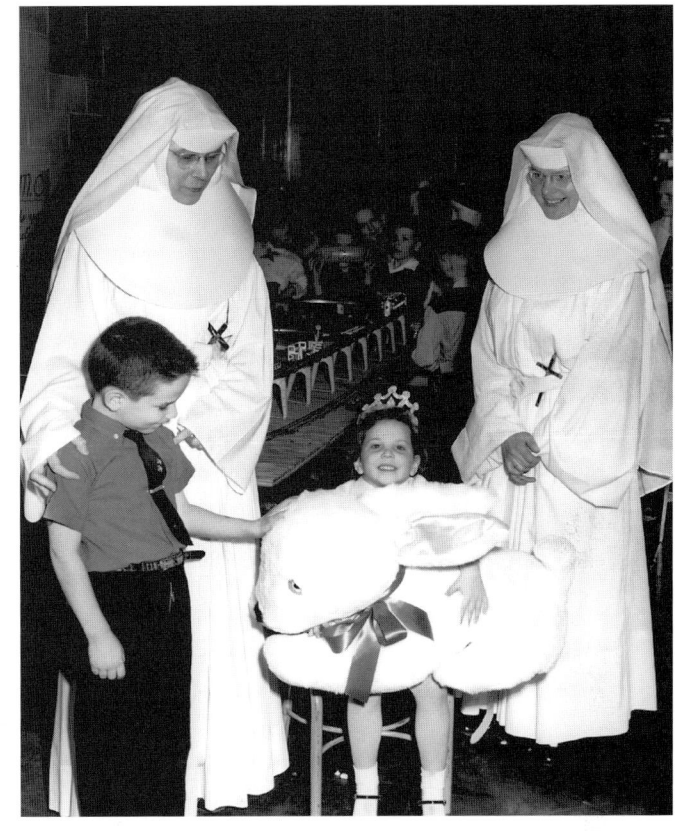

The Ursulines of Ascension wore the white habits of the missionary sisters of their order for Mission Day 1960.

Monsignor Fitzgerald and other parishioners joined village officials in visiting blocks where African American families were

Chapter Four: Monsignor John D. Fitzgerald

Dennis Walsh ('63), pictured with Mother Lucilla, eighth-grade teacher, received a first place award in an essay contest sponsored by the Catholic War Veterans, presented by Joseph Vadovicky.

planning to move. They worked to calm fears and rumors, and identified those white families on the block that could take block leadership roles to address neighbors' concerns. The result was the landmark Fair Housing Act, passed in 1968. Parishioners John Gearen and Frank Muriello were actively engaged in formulating the open housing ordinance. For Ascension and Oak Park, the struggle for a Christian response to a changing social reality was difficult and divisive, but one that resulted in a richer, multicultural Oak Park community and embodied Pope John XXIII's call for the Church to be immersed in the modern world.

Societal challenges were not limited to racial relations. The early 1970s were marked by a highly unpopular war that gave rise to student protests and marches. Drug abuse was rampant, crossing all socio-economic classes. An American president was forced to resign. Finally, the United States pulled out of Vietnam, resulting in one of the largest refugee crises in history. One hundred and forty thousand Vietnamese refugees fled to the United States, overwhelming the resources of resettlement agencies. Ascension was one of the many Catholic parishes nationwide that volunteered to resettle a Vietnamese refugee family. Parishioners helped the newest Americans with food, clothing, housing, and job assistance.

Ascensionites also took the lead in addressing another societal problem—senior citizens losing their homes owing to increased taxes or unanticipated expenses. Older members of the parish had formed the Golden Domers in 1971. Although mostly social in nature, with activities such as

> *When I started at Ascension in the '60s, you roller skated in the gym and watched boxing matches. When I graduated in 1970, you attended "guitar Mass" in the gym. What a difference a decade makes!*
>
> ✣ *Anonymous*

luncheons and card parties, the Golden Domers were also involved in social issues. Some of the Golden Domers joined the Grey Panthers, a national organization of senior citizens committed to the needs of the elderly. Some of Ascension's Golden Domers/Grey Panthers led a push for affordable housing in Oak Park. The results were the construction of the Mills Park Tower in 1975 and subsidized rents funded in part by the Department of Housing and Urban Development.

At Ascension, community building proved to be the mortar that kept the parish together. A big boost to community came in the form of the choir. In 1969, women were invited to join the previously all-male choir. Prior to the admission of women, the male choir practiced on Friday nights. High attendance was guaranteed; following choir practice, the men were invited to the Pine Room for cards, and the boys enjoyed exclusive playing time in "open gym." With the admission of women to the choir, the music ministry at Ascension embarked on a remarkable and highly successful path.

In 1973, Monsignor Fitzgerald retired, and the parish leadership shifted to Father Bernard White, who had served as an assistant priest in the parish earlier in Monsignor Fitzgerald's time. Monsignor Fitzgerald became pastor emeritus and lived in the rectory. He died in November 1984 and was buried from Ascension Parish. Monsignor Fitzgerald was known at Ascension and in the Archdiocese of Chicago for his wit and keen intellect. Mostly, however, he is known for leading Ascension through some of its most challenging years. ✟

Nativity scene in front of Mary's altar before the church was repainted for the fiftieth anniversary of the parish.

Chapter Four: Monsignor John D. Fitzgerald

CHAPTER FIVE

Father Bernard White

1973–1980

Father Bernard White had been an assistant pastor under Monsignor Fitzgerald and was chosen to succeed him upon Monsignor Fitzgerald's retirement in 1973. When he returned to Ascension, it was not considered a prestigious appointment. Oak Park was engulfed in turmoil, and the mood in South Oak Park was not positive. The village economy was shifting because of the movement of auto dealers and large retail outlets out of the village. The conversion of many old buildings into condominiums brought more cars into the neighborhoods, and off-street parking was challenging. Housing costs were low as fear of racial change led some residents to leave the area. Ascension's parish enrollment dropped from 2,500 families to 1,900 families between 1971 and 1975.

Continuity and Transition

Father White was replacing a pastor who had served for twenty-two years, and he was assuming responsibility for buildings that had been heavily used for decades. He was sure when he returned to Oak Park as a pastor that the changes in the community and in the church were going to provide him with great challenges. He was not mistaken. But the continuity of the parish family helped transcend some of the problems that the parish was facing.

Community Mass in the gym was so large and noisy you needed a microphone to be heard during the dialogue homily. The dialogue homily—wow! What a great exchange of ideas and affirming of our faith.

✣ *Mary Schaal*

Father White guided the parish through the continued changes wrought by Vatican II, increasing the presence of the laity in liturgy and in church administration. The priest literally turned toward the people and invited them to participate in the church. One of the Ursuline Sisters who served at Ascension during the seventies said, "It is true that vocations began to decline about the same time that the laity became more involved with the church. We've always seen the decline as a sad time, but, really, we should look at it the other way. We're *all* invited to live as people of God and to serve each other and the church. It is a way for the church to grow, not shrink."

Father White, a Bing Crosby look-alike with a great singing voice himself, worked as a guidance counselor at St. Ignatius College

Prep High School in addition to his pastoral duties. His work with young people was important to him, and young people responded warmly.

A bit of infamy for the parish occurred in 1973 when Oak Park, having been "dry" for one hundred years, began granting liquor licenses. Ascension received the first one. A group of parishioners approached an assistant pastor during Father White's absence, seeking permission to apply for the license. Not realizing the weight of the issue, he granted permission. When the license was issued, the news made the *Chicago Tribune*, much to the pastor's chagrin. But Ascension had a very popular beer garden for the annual "Day in Our Village" celebration.

Ascension and Ascension's parish leadership became involved in local activism. Community groups often used parish facilities for meetings. Parish clergy became active in the Oak Park Community Welfare Council, an organization funded by Community Chest that oversees the coordination of community services. Many of the citizens who were instrumental in helping lead Oak Park through the turmoil of the 1970s were Ascension parishioners.

School enrollment had begun to decline a decade earlier, having peaked in 1963 at over 1,200 students. Ascension had fewer really large families than in the 1950s, and tuition was rising with the increased cost of salaries for lay teachers. In 1977, 493 children were enrolled in school and more than 500 in the Religious Education program. Ascension faced the same concern that many other parishes were facing: How do you maintain a parish school with ever-increasing costs? The newly formed school board, with the help of many active school parents, led the search for solutions at Ascension. These groups investigated the use of some public school resources to help with the math and science curricula but ultimately decided against that collaboration. With increased parental involvement in the administration of the school came increased conflict. The

For many years, Bud Hughes opened and locked the church daily. Photo dated 1979.

Father White celebrates Christmas in the convent.

Members of the class of 1979, with their ribbons.

> *In the 1970s, you could still play dodge ball during gym class. I still have a strong memory of Chip Pollard's powerful arm—what a feat to catch his shot and knock him out.*
>
> ✝ *Brooker Granholm*

significant investment of family resources for tuition led to concern about the quality of education.

In a project designed to raise money for the parish, lift spirits, and foster a good time, the Altar and Rosary Society began producing musicals each spring, starting in 1976. They also held rummage sales, card parties, fashion shows, and luncheons; "pantry showers" helped fill the kitchen cupboards of the convent. In 1979, Altar and Rosary held the first "Holiday Fare," a Christmas boutique for the community beyond Ascension. But it was the musicals that became the center of Ascension's social life and perhaps helped hold the parish together through the next sixteen years.

A Report Card to Be Proud of

In 1980, Father White could no longer ignore his failing health and moved to a less polluted area and a milder climate: Santa Rosa, California. In an interview before he left, he told a reporter for the *Wednesday Journal*, "I am on loan to them. I'm going out to try it. I can leave at any time. This was a tremendous decision. The biggest one I've made since my ordination to the priesthood."

Looking back on those years, it is easy to imagine the toll this assignment took on his health. Father White's years at Ascension were intense ones. He is one of the few remaining clergy who remembers when he was called a curate rather than an associate pastor. He had that role with Monsignor Fitzgerald and is quick to admit that the Monsignor was a tough act to follow when he took over the pastorate. But follow it he did, both in plant improvements and program development.

Perhaps his greatest memorial, though, is a memorial to change. In his tenure, the results of Vatican II

The new altar for the fiftieth anniversary of the church, 1979.

The celebration of the fiftieth anniversary of the building of the church.

The congregation for the jubilee Mass. The banner on the loft is the coat of arms of Pope John Paul II.

Chapter Five: Father Bernard White

The Ursulines who taught at Ascension in 1978.

were filtering down to the parishes. Lay people, who had always done the work, now took on responsibility and leadership. Father White often had to walk the tightrope between change and continuity with the past, and he became an accomplished aerial artist.

It is safe to say that not everybody always agreed with his decisions. Most daringly, he appointed laywomen to positions of responsibility, which put him well ahead of the institutional church. Whatever the tensions, during his tenure, Ascension was one of the parishes where seminarians were sent to learn what the real world was going to be like after ordination. He helped prepare them for the tightrope act and did it with good grace. Father White's report card has a lot of A's on it. ✣

> *In the mid-1970s, the Christian Family Movement sponsored two large Vietnamese families. CFM got them housing, furniture, food, and jobs.*
>
> ✣ *Anonymous*

Gym Mass

✠

Vatican II called for many changes in the liturgy, and a great deal of leeway in the implementation of those changes was given in the days after the Council. The guitar Mass was one very popular result of that change; dialogue homilies fit nicely with the relaxed ceremony, and increased involvement by the laity brought new energy and creativity to the liturgy. Many of these folks went on to become ministerial leaders in the "big church."

At Ascension, the gym Mass (also known as the 10:00 Mass, the folk Mass, the guitar Mass, or the family Mass) began in the late 1960s as an attempt by members of CFM (Christian Family Movement) to create a Mass that would be meaningful to families. Father Fitzgerald accommodated the group and, though he never said Mass in the gym himself, encouraged those who helped plan the weekly gatherings. Over the years, many school families became involved as well through the Home and School Association, and the Family School (an early version of our Religious Ed program) evolved.

In the early years, hundreds would attend the Mass and would sit in chairs and in the bleachers that were set up along the north and south walls of the gym. Individuals were responsible for planning and setting up for the liturgies; later on, liturgy teams were formed and were part of the parish liturgy committee. The team held the responsibility for carrying out the liturgy and for baking the communion bread, making changes in the environment (including banners, which figured largely in the Mass), post-communion meditation, special handouts, dramatizations, and special opportunities for the children to become involved.

A key feature of the 10:00 Mass was the dialogue homily. It was an opportunity for the congregation to say how their life experiences reflected the topic in the homily or the readings. One participant remembers, "The hand of the Holy Spirit was unmistakable in many of these sharings." Refreshments were served after the Mass, and this sharing continued long after "The Mass has ended; let us go in peace." (Can you imagine Mass lasting more than an hour and a half and no one complaining?)

The priests who led the liturgies tended to be the young assistants: Fathers La Range, Prichard, Voss, Hickey, Poplis, and Joyce. Visitors were taken (and sometimes shaken!) by the energy, the music, and sometimes the dance and drama of the gym Mass.

Changes had taken place in the Mass in the "big church," too, though, and people began moving back to those liturgies. Other families moved out of the parish. To maintain some of the intimacy of the service as the crowd diminished, the 10:00 Mass moved into the Pine Room. The community changed gradually to younger families, and the liturgy changed to accommodate them.

In 1998, because of the declining priest population in the parish, the Mass was discontinued, but the 10:00 crowd remained committed to their community. They developed the "Extending the Word" ministry, which still meets every Sunday following the 9:00 Mass for song, prayer, and fellowship.

The Shows

A 1976 *Dome* article announced that the Altar and Rosary Society would hold auditions for a musical variety show. Parishioners were excited. Laurel Cronin, an Oak Park actress and Ascension neighbor, was to direct. Direct she did! She cast the show, designed the costumes, and taught the dance steps that year (*The Spirit of '76*) and the next (*Cabaret USA*). Laurel became well known in the Chicago theatrical community and was headed to New York with the touring production of *Annie* when she became ill and died at a tragically young age.

In 1978, Bob Wright took on the show's direction. Bob had directed a theatrical group at St. Bernardine Parish, as well as shows at Village Players. A wonderfully talented writer and director, Bob headed the Ascension shows from 1978 until 1991. He wrote each show, chose the music, and recruited musicians for the production. Years later, Bob said, "I was not only accepted but I immediately felt a caring, loving warmth. Friendships grew then that are a cherished part of my life. God knew what he was doing when he led me to Ascension."

At the same time, Lynn Kirsch joined the production team as choreographer, and during the years that followed, Lynn, too, became a much-loved honorary Ascensionite. A professionally trained dancer, Lynn welcomed all comers. She started with basics and helped us to tap our toes with the best of them. Then, as now, it was difficult to find available space on our campus, so we often found ourselves tapping in our kitchens or in someone's basement or attic.

During the first years of the show, there was no stage curtain. Scene changes were accomplished by moving the spotlight to the opposite side of the bare-bones stage where the actors were performing a skit. Our first stage was like a collection of collapsible serving tables. It was fine for skits with two or three actors, or for solos and small-group singing numbers. Dance numbers, on the other hand, were a little tricky. There were times when we were tapping on top while stalwart souls were on their backs with their feet up bracing the underside of the stage. At a dress rehearsal one year, a crew member noticed these stalwart souls and said, "This will never happen again. I'll build you a stage."

Thus, a stage committee of volunteer carpenters was assembled, and a real, solid stage began to take shape. Over the course of several years, it grew from a single level four feet off the ground to a variety of levels of varying sizes, sometimes with ramps and runways. The cast would start each new show's rehearsals wondering what Bob and his carpenters were adding to the stage this time!

We were on a slim-to-nothing budget, so our costumers had to be extremely creative. For some numbers, Bob would simply tell us what attitude or era the numbers were portraying; it was up to us to assemble our own costumes, resulting in trips to the Salvation Army Store and the Economy Shop. But certain numbers needed specific costumes, and our costume crew always came through. Many talented seamstresses in the parish suffered from eyestrain getting us all ready for the productions.

We produced shows at Ascension for three reasons: fellowship, fund-raising, and fun during the long, dull days

One of Ascension's first shows: The Spirit of '76.

of winter. We accomplished all of these aims, and all kinds of people came. People who had known Ascension only through its weekend Masses joined the cast and met parishioners who were active in other parish ministries: choir, Altar and Rosary, Holy Name Society, School Board, ushers, Ministers of Care—many newcomers went on to join and enrich those ministries. The cast usually numbered between fifty and seventy-five, but one year it topped one hundred. In the last years of the show, the number of behind-the-scenes workers was well over one hundred.

Grade-school students could help with props and "go-fer" tasks; when they reached high school, they could be part of the cast. It was delightful to watch the young people grow up with the show. Some who started out as page-turners for the pianist or as mike-movers or prop kids became vocalists or dancers in high school or college.

Auditions were held around Halloween, and rehearsals began in mid-November. Rehearsals for solos and small group numbers were held three evenings a week in the Pine Room. If you were in a variety of numbers, you spent a lot of winter hours in the Pine Room! Some brought knitting, reading material, and even bills to pay while waiting to rehearse their next number.

On Sunday afternoons, the whole cast assembled to rehearse the large ensemble pieces. It was on Sunday afternoon that our "food angel" would often appear. Mildred McDonald would arrive with beautifully arranged baskets of fruit, cheese, and sweets for the cast and crew to nibble when they weren't on stage. Others took their cue from Mildred and brought goodies to share—sometimes delicious leftovers from Saturday night parties. On show weekends, Mildred became the "bathroom angel," appointing herself a committee of one to dress up the restrooms in the Pine Room and the gym.

Troupers Mary McEnery and Kathleen Kernan, 1987.

Director Bob Wright shares a moment with trouper Marilyn Trainor.

The leisurely winter months of rehearsing were followed by the grind of production week in mid-February. During this week, it became obvious where the weaknesses in the show were: group numbers that needed work, costumes that didn't fit or didn't show up well under the lights, props that were missing. It sometimes took long hours to resolve these problems, but resolved they were, and, as opening night approached, spirits improved and nerves quieted.

The show ran for two weekends. The first Friday, opening night, everyone arrived well ahead of time. The men's dressing room was the gym locker room. The women's dressing room was the second floor O'Keefe room (known in different generations as the canteen, the science room, or the extended day room). Quick changes, though, with no time to make it all the way to the dressing room and back, had to be done in stairwells. It was crowded but fun; everyone shared the space available, swapped jewelry, helped with zippers and snaps, and soothed frayed nerves.

Late in the afternoon before the Saturday performances, the entire production staff gathered before a portable altar placed before the stage and celebrated Mass—a very meaningful way to strengthen our community. A few minutes before the overture began, we gathered again for a prayer to St. Genesius, the patron saint of actors.

Ascension's final show was produced in 1991, but the friendships made during sixteen years "on the boards" continue to enrich our parish life and parish ministries. People came just wanting to be in the large group numbers and discovered

The program cover for an Ascension show, Cabaret USA, *1977.*

latent talents for singing and dancing and acting. People came back to the church. People got married. People died. And those grieving were comforted and supported by fellow cast members. People let go of disagreements for the sheer pleasure of working together on a wonderful project.

One longtime cast member writes, "When we reminisce about the shows, we fully realize how unique those times were. Those days were filled with fun, laughter, songs, camaraderie, and the wonderful Ascension people who entered our lives." Another adds, "I can't describe the feeling of belonging to a group working together for a common goal . . . the feeling of joy in watching people grow in self-confidence. The feeling of pride in a job well done . . . and the pure and simple feeling of having fun!"

Jane Drake and Tom Hughes, "A Couple of Swells."

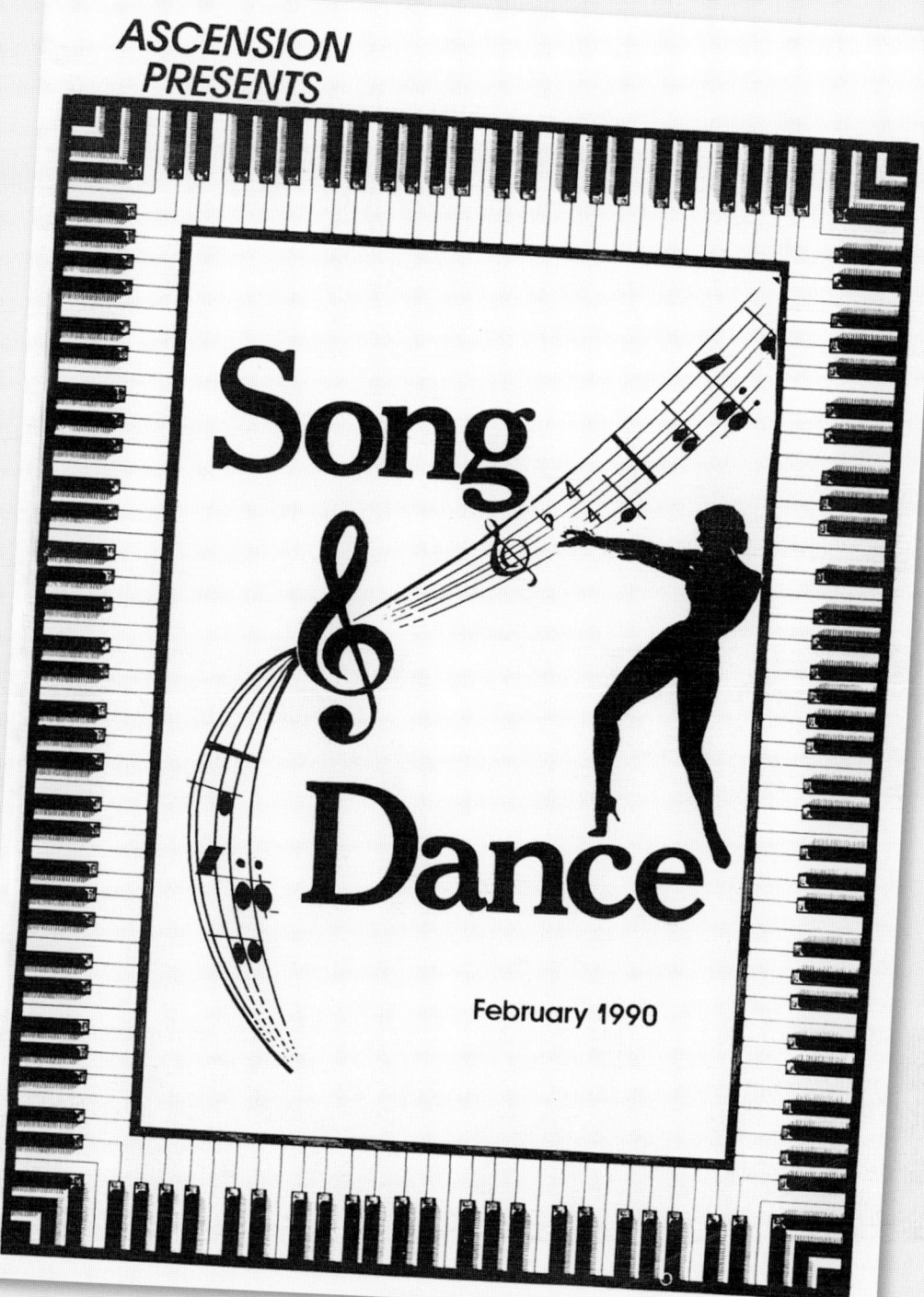

Father Gerard Broccolo

Father Robert Cross

CHAPTER SIX

Father Gerard T. Broccolo
Father Robert Cross

1980–1988

Father Gerard T. (Jerry) Broccolo came to Ascension on the Feast of Christ the King, November 23, 1980, and left on June 30, 1982. Before Ascension, Father Broccolo worked at the Office of Divine Worship for the archdiocese. Father Broccolo's tenure at Ascension turned out to be a brief bridge between the Father White and the Father Cross years, but during his time, Ascension continued to change. When he left Ascension, Father Broccolo returned to a lay ministry training program and eventually worked in health care administration.

Father Broccolo remembers his brief time in Oak Park:

> I struggled with the idea that this was a pastor's parish; I was interested in less of a "me" and more of a "we." I promoted collaborative models of church ministry within the parish and in Oak Park. It was while I was at Ascension that I had one of my best ecumenical experiences. We had a very active group of clergy from different denominations in the community. We had a pulpit-sharing group, so we actually would preach at each other's churches. For a time we met every Friday morning for two or two and a half hours. The time together included prayer, an

> *Christ Renews His Parish was formed, where twenty to thirty men, then women, would have a weekend to be renewed by listening to our stories, reflecting on it, and looking to change our lives.*
> ☩ *Anonymous*

update on community news and then we would prepare our homilies together. There were twenty or so ministers involved—I was the only Catholic priest—and we put forth a coordinated effort to preach the same message.

If there was a hallmark of that short time, it was the collaborative model. We had a large group in the parish, not a parish council, a larger group than that. It was sort of an umbrella group that asked, "What is going on? What are we trying to achieve? How are we doing?"

An evangelization group called Outreach developed at Ascension during this period. Outreach sought to include anyone marginalized, left out, disenfranchised, or lost in the Ascension community. Beyond welcoming these people, Outreach went to find them and invite their participation in parish life. Block captains organized the effort. Some who were found by Outreach volunteers have remained at Ascension ever since.

Father Robert Cross

Ascension celebrated its Seventy-fifth Jubilee on October 3, 1982. Volunteers designed new banners for the church, sewn in pieces that look like bricks, each brick representing a family in the Ascension community.

Although it had already been announced that Father Robert Cross would be the new pastor of Ascension, he had not yet arrived at the parish. Technically, Ascension was without a pastor for this occasion for its Jubilee, so Bishop William E. McManus, member of the Ascension class of 1938, was the main celebrant of the Mass, concelebrating with the assistants who were serving at the time, including Father Paul Beno, who was also serving as the parish administrator between pastors. A special liturgy was held, followed by a celebration in the gym and the courtyard. Bishop McManus's homily was printed in its entirety in the *Dome* a few weeks later. It included these thoughts:

Ed Kane: A Simple Man Who Touched Many Young Lives

✠

Every day, Ed Kane cleaned Ascension Church. That's what he did. That's what he told everybody he did.

"Clean church every day," he said as he extended his hand to you.

He was good at his work, and he was proud of it. The work gave him a sense of purpose and a place to go each morning.

It was when he didn't come to work, when he didn't come to the mass which always preceded his day's work, that people worried and called for him at the Oak Park Arms where he had lived in recent years.

Ed Kane had died in the night, quietly. He was 67 years old.

While he died on July 19, in some way, Ed Kane was not laid to rest until a week or so ago when the children of Ascension School, children he knew by name, came together to acknowledge his passing and their loss.

"Ed was so important to the whole school community," said the Rev. Robert Cross, pastor of Ascension parish. "The children had many memories of him. He was very affectionate with the kids. He said, 'Hello,' and was always shaking their hands. He knew them and they appreciated that. Since he died over the summer when the kids were away from school, we wanted to have a time to all get together and mark this."

The occasion was a prayer liturgy on a Friday afternoon in late September. The younger grade school children drew pictures and wrote a short sentence or two about Ed Kane. The pictures were of rainbows and balloons, doves and hearts. The phrases told of a man who had had a simple but very direct impact on a lot of young lives.

"Ed was a very nice man," wrote one young girl. "If he saw you, he would shake your hand and smile. Dear Ed, rest in peace." Another wrote, "Ed was a very special person to the parish. He liked the kids a lot, too. The church won't be the same without Ed." One child looked ahead. "Ed, I hope you are as happy up in heaven as you were here!"

Dan Haley
Wednesday Journal
October 10, 1984

For three quarters of a century, Ascension Parish, year after year, decade after decade, has anticipated the future, planned for it, and adjusted to it. Unlike some other parishes, which, unprepared for the future, were tossed about and tormented by it, even ruined by it, Ascension has weathered the storms of demographic, cultural, and economic change, never panicking, never losing its cool or its courage.

I have known all six of Ascension's pastors before Father Cross, and I know him well, too, and all were men who looked ahead, figured out the parish's future needs, confidently plunged into projects to fulfill them like trustworthy captains of a ship, they stuck to their post on the bridge when the ship sailed through wars, depressions, changes in the neighborhood, and upheavals in the church.

So my friends, here, in summary is what lies ahead for Ascension. All are called and commissioned by Jesus Christ to fill this whole parish—the neighborhood, church, school, rectory, convent, and hall—to fill it all with the presence of the Lord.

Musicians sing for a wedding, 1983.

Father Robert Cross was installed as Ascension's seventh pastor on October 23, 1982. He came to Ascension from Our Lady of Lourdes in the inner city following eighteen years of teaching at Quigley Seminary. Father Cross had earned a master's degree in library science from Rosary College (now Dominican University) and is also, in his own words, "a master of the semi-colon!" When Father Broccolo left Ascension, Cardinal Bernardin, in his first appointment, asked Father Cross to take the parish. Father Cross remembers, "Oak Park was changing and they wanted someone who had experience with a racially diverse parish. I asked my nephew, Tom McGrath—a member of Ascension's finance committee—if the parish was a good fit for me and he encouraged me to come." Father Cross's warm, simple notes in the *Dome* suggested someone who enjoyed his assignment very much. Chatty and casual, Father Cross's communiqués told about his easy acceptance in the parish.

Kenny Burns, Ascension class of 2002, at his baptism, October 1988, with his parents and godparents and Father Leon Rezula.

His administration, though, was to handle even more internal change than his predecessor's. Tuition for the school continued to rise, and enrollment continued to drop. In fall of 1982, Sponsor-A-Student was born, a program through which parishioners could help school parents who were struggling with tuition payments. In February 1984, Sister Theresa Davy announced that she would be leaving her position as Ascension School's principal. Although the search committee interviewed seven candidates to replace her, no religious sisters applied for the position. Dave Grayson was hired, the first lay person to lead the school in its seventy-three-year history. The following year, the Ursulines announced their impending departure from Ascension. Father Paul Beno left Ascension in April 1984 after six years as an assistant and administrator; when he left, the 7:30 a.m. Mass was taken off the daily schedule.

Father Cross was committed to justice issues and was frank in his support of such hot-button topics as the pending handgun ban

The Peace and Justice Committee

The Peace and Justice Committee (P&J) at Ascension started in the spring of 1983, when Father Bob Cross settled in as pastor. At the time, the American bishops were addressing major social justice issues, such as the nuclear arms race and a just American economy.

Ascension had already had a long history of social justice activity. The Saint Vincent de Paul Society had worked on behalf of the poor for many decades, and Ascension's role as a sharing parish with St. Mel on the West Side of Chicago reinforced that work. In the 1960s, Ascension parishioners played a significant role in the issue of housing integration in Oak Park. During the 1970s, many Ascension members were engaged in social justice issues through outside groups, such as Chicago Call to Action, CISPES (Committee in Solidarity with the People of El Salvador), and the Pledge of Resistance.

The creation of an official committee at Ascension in 1983 put the stamp of the parish on the work in which we were engaged. The purpose of P&J was to initiate our own efforts while continuing to support those of others. Other parishes started P&J groups about this time, but Ascension's P&J is one of the longest continuous efforts in the Archdiocese.

P&J differed from similar programs in the parish in two ways. First, it was built explicitly on the encyclicals of the Church that emphasized justice rather than service. Second, it engaged in actions in the public realm to bring about social change.

Much of our early work tracked the American bishops' approach to problems of national and international significance. Ascension acted in coalition with many other groups engaged in these efforts. Internally, P&J focused on a two-part approach in its work: education and action. One of our early educational efforts was to form study groups that read and discussed the social encyclicals. These educational efforts were supplemented by experts who would join us to lead our discussion. Among many speakers, P&J invited Professor Michael Schuck of Loyola University to speak on the history of social encyclicals and Professor Richard Woods, O.P., from Dominican University to speak on the pre-war situation in Iraq.

As part of the early efforts, Father Cross preached on social justice issues in his Sunday homilies. While these public statements were not appreciated by all parishioners—and sometimes P&J got blamed for instigating them—they gave public notice of the fact that social justice was a constitutive part of the Gospel. Sometimes issues became too divisive to be embraced by our agenda, though our members could pursue their work on them by collaborating with groups outside the parish.

P&J has never been a large membership organization, but it has been a consistent one, and we have always had a constituency of supporters beyond our membership. Thus, P&J has been the voice of social justice in the parish. That voice has found expression through the *Dome*, study groups, speakers, notices of conferences, and rallies sponsored by like-minded groups.

While Peace and Justice is not a service organization, it has become the referral point for service projects that parishioners felt would be worthwhile. For example, it is difficult to say how many coats, sweaters, scarves, hats, and socks were collected for the Austin Soup Kitchen clients, but in the mid-1980s, seven or eight carloads were gathered at Ascension and delivered each winter.

Besides education and social action, P&J has consistently tried to develop a justice formation sense both within the group and in the parish. For many years, P&J sponsored a church service to celebrate Martin Luther King Day. We conducted overnight or daylong retreats for members that strove to put justice into the context of the Gospels. Since the 1990s, we have always reserved the first portion of our meeting for a reflection on Scripture or other sources of inspiration.

P&J sponsors ongoing programs, such as the CROP (Church World Service) Hunger Walk since 1986; Good Friday Walk for Justice (Eighth Day Center) since 1985; Candidates' Night for Village Trustees from 1985 to 2003. Certain issues have persisted for a number of years. For example, the U.S. policy in Central America was an over-riding P&J concern in the 1980s. In the 1990s, homelessness and welfare reform were abiding issues. Ascension became involved with PADS (Public Action to Deliver Shelter) first as a possible site and then as a major recruiter of volunteer workers. The new century has had P&J involved in death penalty work on a consistent basis, including collecting signatures in collaboration with the Illinois Coalition to Abolish the Death Penalty. Finally, the war in Iraq has been a particular focus of P&J since 2003.

Over the years, Ascension has been associated with many outside groups and their issues. UPAJ (United Power for Action and Justice) is a broad-based amalgam of organizations that Ascension Parish joined in 1998. There are about ten church-related organizations in the Oak Park area that are UPAJ members. Ascension P&J members have acted in coalition with them in actions for health care, housing, gun control, and immigration. Among our local partners are Good Shepherd Lutheran, Oak Park Temple, St. Giles, St. Luke, Grace Lutheran, and the five Catholic churches in Berwyn/Cicero's Interfaith Leadership Project.

Many Ascensionites have been active members of P&J since its inception. Their voices resound in calling all believers to action on issues of justice.

Patrick McAnany

in Oak Park. His letters to the parish included advocacy of the hunger walks in Oak Park, jobs for political refugees, fair housing for all citizens, and boycotts of products that were harmful to developing countries. Some issues brought the parish together in solidarity; some, however, divided the parish. This division over political issues, school personnel and policy, and ministry to the extended community was to remain a part of Ascension culture into the early years of the next century.

The interdenominational group with whom Father Broccolo met invited Father Cross to join them, meeting weekly and sharing a lectionary. Father Cross "learned a lot of scripture" and continues to meet with the group at Austin Boulevard Christian Church.

Father Cross brought Christ Renews His Parish (CRHP) to Ascension in 1984. CRHP was a retreat-based program that encouraged groups to spend time away in meditation, prayer, and contemplation of their role in Christ's church. Groups of men began

Members of the class of 1936 at their fifty-first reunion.

their weekends of formation early in 1984. Women's groups began to develop in the fall of that year. CRHP encouraged both interior spiritual renewal and the call to minister to others in the community. It helped to build other programs that were responsible for the steadily increasing involvement of the laity in the church leadership: Theology on Tap, Backyard Theology, the Christian Family Movement (CFM), Theology for Homemakers, and Bible Studies. His pastorate also saw the beginning of RCIA (Rite of Christian Initiation of Adults), a major program for evangelization.

Father Cross completed his time as pastor of Ascension in 1988. He says, "My blood pressure was high, and my doctor suggested that being a pastor was not good for my blood pressure. I became an assistant at St. Cornelius, took a pill, and my blood pressure came down!" In his last letter in the *Dome* he shared these thoughts:

Ursuline sisters in Ascension convent, 1980s.

> I will miss writing this letter.
> I will miss having dessert with the Golden Domers.
> I will miss bowling with the Holy Name Men.
> I will miss women cleaning up the church on Fridays.
> I will miss saying the Rosary before the 8:15 Mass.
> I will miss accepting big checks from the A & R at their luncheons.
> I will miss half-hour St. Vincent de Paul meetings.
> I will miss Backyard Theology.
> I will miss writing and reading HELP letters on CRHP.
> I will miss watching the Ascension Chargers playing basketball.
> I will miss saying Mass under the Dome.
> I will miss the blossoming trees in front of the Rectory.
> I will miss the beautiful children of Ascension.
> I will miss you.

A Brief History of Religious Education at Ascension

Someone looking for the newly created Religious Education office in 1973 would have been directed to the little room off the gym entrance, across from the library—currently the athletic director's office. Associate Pastor Father Tom Hickey had just hired Anna Sokolofski to coordinate the CCD (Confraternity of Christian Doctrine) program. She was the first layperson to hold this position. Before she was hired, classes had always been administered by the principal of Ascension School.

Lorraine Manahan, and then Bernadette Dehn, succeeded Anna. Kay Brennan served as secretary for both. Father White hired the next coordinator, Sister Maureen Cleary, BVM. Under Sister Maureen's leadership, classes moved from Saturday mornings to Tuesday evenings. The office was then located in Room 103 of the school. To enhance the program, she offered an art guild and a music workshop, both of which met before CCD sessions.

In fall of 1983, Sister Maureen became very ill but continued to work as she was able. On the night of Confirmation, which was held in February, there was a heavy snowstorm. Her colleagues encouraged Sister Maureen not to attend the service. She said, "This is the work I love. If I die doing it, that would be a good way to die." Soon afterward, she was hospitalized. She spent several days in intensive care and died on the eve of the Annunciation, March 24, 1984, surrounded by the Sisters of her community praying the rosary. Her funeral was held at Ascension, and many children mourned her passing. A lilac bush next to the statue of the Blessed Mother in the rectory yard was dedicated to her memory that spring.

Father Cross hired Sister Maureen's replacement. He changed the title from coordinator to director and expanded the responsibilities dramatically. He wanted someone to do the job of educating parishioners, in his words, "from womb to tomb." Sister Felicia Wolf, SSF, fit the bill. As director of all Religious Education programs in the parish, she directed coordinators of baptismal prep, preschool, religious education, youth ministry, and RCIA. Her secretary at the time was a

Cardinal Bernardin visited the Religious Ed third grade class in 1995.

The Religious Education program prepares all the children of the parish for sacraments. Second graders bake bread before First Eucharist.

Eighth grade students re-enact the Last Supper for Ascension Triduum services. Photo dated 2006. *Father Larry McNally and a first communicant.*

The Religious Ed pumpkin sale.

little-known newcomer to Ascension by the name of Christine Ondrla. Felicia introduced many changes to the program, including the way students were prepared for Confirmation. It was a tumultuous time. For several years, two Confirmation dates were offered to the families of Ascension: one in the parish and one downtown. In the last two years of Sister Felicia's tenure, Mary McEnery became the Religious Education secretary.

In 1989, Sister Felicia left Ascension, and Father Jenks hired me to be the Director of Religious Education. The year I took this position was the first year Ascension opened its doors without an Ursuline on staff. The school and religious education program were both headed by lay administrators. The staff configuration changed yet again. Father Jenks had a staff in which the directors of RCIA, youth ministry, and religious education each reported directly to the pastor. Classes continued on Tuesday evenings, and a Sunday morning option was

Confirmands on retreat before their confirmation. Photo dated October 1996.

added. The Catechesis of the Good Shepherd, a Montessori-based program, was introduced in 1999; in 2004, we added a Wednesday afternoon program specifically so that we could offer all three levels of this fine program.

The Religious Education office has moved several times during my tenure—from Room 103 to Room 104 to 111. After H.O.M.E. (a residential program for senior citizens) moved out of the old convent building, the Religious Education office moved in, where it remains to this day. We had a lovely office in a very quiet building until the rest of the parish offices moved across the street to join us in 2006. Now we have a lovely office in a very busy place. Kathy Marifjeren is the current office administrator.

The history of the program describes the leadership changes, but to tell you where we had our files and who answered the phone doesn't tell you much about the program. The heart of the program has been and will remain the beautiful children who pass through it. It has been the privilege and the blessing of all the women mentioned above, along with the hundreds of catechists who have volunteered in the program, to share their faith with the families of Ascension. May God continue to bless this good work.

Christine Ondrla
Director of Religious Education

School Christmas prayer service.

CHAPTER SEVEN

Father Francis C. Jenks

1988–2003

Following the transfer of Father Robert Cross to a new parish, Father Frank Jenks was installed as Ascension's eighth pastor at the Saturday evening Mass on May 21, 1988. An excellent homilist, a fine singer, and a native of the South Side, Father Jenks was ordained in 1970 and had served at Our Lady of the Wayside Parish in Arlington Heights, at Our Lady of Perpetual Help Parish in Glenview, and at St. Mary of Vernon in Vernon Hills. In his first letter "From the Pastor's Desk" in the May 15, 1988, *Dome*, Father Jenks wrote, "My fondest hope is that, together, we can take the great tradition of Ascension Parish and work together to build the Church of the future."

The day after Father Jenks' arrival, Father Jerry Joyce, who had been a resident at Ascension for seventeen years, was transferred to a parish in Westchester. Associate Pastor Father Leon Rezula celebrated his farewell Mass in June 1990, and the following October, Father Steve Dohner, who had resided at Ascension, returned to his home diocese to work with Catholic Charities in Cleveland. Father Tom Baldonieri joined the parish staff shortly after his ordination in

May 1990. Thus, in the first three years of his pastorate, Father Jenks witnessed the reduction of priests residing in the rectory from four to two. Not long afterward, though, Father Hal Stanger, who worked in vocations for the archdiocese and as a fire chaplain, moved in and assisted with Sunday liturgies.

The long-predicted shortage of priests to serve in Catholic parishes was beginning to become a reality for Ascension Parish. The future had arrived. Father Jenks saw this as a call for more lay leadership and responsibility for both the day-to-day operations of the church and its ministries. The pastorate of Father Jenks was shaped by his response to this call.

The inaugural meeting of Ascension's first Parish Pastoral Council was held September 8, 1991. The council was formed by gathering the leadership of existing parish groups into commissions. Each commission discerned a member to represent them on the council. When Father Jenks reflected later on his first five years at Ascension, he said that the formation of a Parish Pastoral Council was one of the accomplishments in which he took the most pride.

All of Ascension's buildings saw major work during Father Jenks' time as pastor.

PADS

✠

In the fall of 1992, Father Jenks wrote in *The Dome* of the 50 percent growth in requests for shelter services in the Oak Park/River Forest/Forest Park area between 1989 and 1991. Tri-Village PADS (Public Action to Deliver Shelter) was a new outreach program of the local Community of Congregations to provide overnight shelter for the homeless in various sites at local congregations from October 1 through April 30. There were four sites that could be open by October 1; the goal was to add sites as quickly as possible to give coverage throughout the week.

Father Jenks called on the Ascension community to become involved immediately by volunteering services, and he called for a serious conversation to be held on other ways in which Ascension could participate. He subsequently presented a set of facts and myths about homelessness to inform the conversation. Even as the conversations took place, individual Ascension parishioners took part in PADS activities. These functions included working at existing PADS sites, transporting mattresses, preparing and transporting food, and laundering and folding bed linens. (Members of the Ascension Fourth Grade Girl Scout Troop spent Saturday mornings in the spring of 1993 doing this.)

When in January of 1993 Cardinal Bernardin praised St. Edmund Parish for becoming an overnight site in Oak Park, Father Jenks was inspired to see if Ascension could become one as well. In February 1993, a committee was formed to explore Ascension's involvement in the Tri-Village PADS project. When the PADS Committee approached him for discussion of the subject, Father Jenks referred the matter to the Parish Pastoral Council. Over the course of many months, discussions took place in many quarters. Participants often held strong views on the subject and expressed those views with conviction.

Father Jenks watched the community becoming polarized over the subject, and he saw little hope that the few people left in the middle could mitigate the polarization. A meeting on the PADS program scheduled for January 27, 1994, was postponed after internal parish communications became public. An all-parish PADS meeting was eventually held on May 9. As a result of that meeting, Father Jenks decided that, for the foreseeable future, Ascension Parish's participation in the program would continue to be through the volunteer efforts of individual Ascension parishioners in existing PADS functions at sites already established. To help cope with the strong feelings brought to the surface by the PADS discussions, the parish held a healing prayer service for the Ascension community on June 23, 1994.

Ten years later, in the fall of 2004, Father Larry McNally was approached with the same question, which he brought to the Parish Pastoral Council. The Council reasoned that, after ten years of seeing what PADS had become, the parish might be ready to consider becoming a site. Hearing sessions were held in November, and, again, strong feelings on both sides left the parish polarized. Father McNally decided, as Father Jenks had, that Ascension would continue to participate through the voluntary participation of parishioners.

During the course of the discussion, though, many people had expressed interest in helping with the homeless situation in other ways. Father McNally invited parishioners to an open meeting to discuss how that might happen. The meeting ended with the parish members expressing a willingness to cooperate with Catholic Charities in supporting an apartment to assist families in need with shelter and a fresh start. The parish's New Hope apartment project has been a source of healing for the parish as well as an opportunity for a new life for several families.

It was the perfect way to move to a parishioner-led parish and a proven consensus-building technique. While decision-making still belonged to the pastor, he now made those decisions after receiving the benefit of the wisdom and experience of the lay leadership of the parish.

Recognizing the need to reduce some of the administrative duties of the pastor and to increase the level of professional management of the parish, Ascension hired a business manager in the mid-1990s. As in many other areas, the responsibility of the business of the parish moved to lay people but not to volunteers. Tom Gull, an active parishioner, was hired; his considerable management and marketing skills helped establish sound business practices for the parish.

Communication between the church and parishioners improved with the redesign of *The Dome* in 1995 and the birth of the parish newsletter. This new venue gave the pastor and pastoral staff expanded opportunities to explain educational, spiritual, and liturgical changes; to offer inspiration and information; and to invite the parish into fuller participation in parish life. The Parish Pastoral Council wrote a mission statement, helping to communicate the vision that they saw for the parish to each parishioner.

A Tradition of Music

The wonderful shows begun in 1976 had run their course by 1991. Volunteers rested briefly and then applied their energies to new programs. The school auction was one event that replaced the social component of the shows and the large-scale volunteer effort that the shows had offered the parish. The first auction,

In 1995, my son Michael broke his neck in a freak accident playing in snow and became a spinal cord injury victim, paralyzed from the waist down. This parish showed its true spirit by rallying around this family with love and support, time and food, and it's been that way before and after. The power of a prayer group cannot be duplicated! Mike has married Jessica and just had a son!

✣ *Rosemarie Nowicki*

Lights, Camera, Auction! was held in 1994. Auctions soon became the biggest social event of the school year, and the profits grew as the event did, starting in the $20,000 range and expanding to nearly $100,000 at the thirteenth auction in 2006.

"Concerts under the Dome," a chamber music series begun in 1991, developed out of the wealth of musical talent in the parish and attracted many people to come to Ascension. One of those concerts featured Father John Moulder, who had become associate pastor at Ascension in July 1995 and was a much-acclaimed jazz guitarist, with seven-time Grammy winner Paul Wertico.

The music ministry at Ascension continued to grow under David Anderson's direction. By the end of the twentieth century, four talented choirs, two adult and two children, were leading Ascension in song. The monthly Taizé prayer service, an ecumenical service of prayer and chant, grew from a few dozen people in 1992 to a full church on the first Friday of each month. In recognition of his leadership of Taizé, David received an award from the Association of Chicago Priests, applauding his outstanding contribution to the life in the church of Chicago.

In October 2001, ninety-two choir members, family members, and friends traveled to Rome and other parts of Italy. Highlights of the tour included singing at Mass at St. Peter's Basilica in the Vatican, a major concert at the Church of Sant'Ignazio (Saint Ignatius) in Rome, a brief concert at the Duomo (cathedral) in Milan, and a private Mass in a chapel of the Basilica of St. Francis in Assisi, with Father Jenks presiding.

Chapter Seven: Father Francis C. Jenks

Refocusing Catholicism

There was a great deal happening in the church of the United States at this time. On the one hand, there was a new spirit in the church, and Cardinal Joseph Bernardin seemed to be the driving force behind it. He introduced himself to the priests of the diocese saying: "I am Joseph, your brother," a statement that proved prophetic. He was embraced by Chicago clergy and their flocks and enjoyed a good reputation in the city of Chicago. He brought a gentle energy to the Cathedral that invigorated his colleagues and brought a sense of optimism to local Catholics.

But at the same time, the church was enduring the investigation of sex abuse cases dating back several decades, and Cardinal Bernardin himself was not free from scrutiny. In 1993, a young man accused him of sexual abuse, and the Cardinal was personally immersed in the nightmare of the scandal. The young man later recanted and apologized to the Cardinal. Cardinal Bernardin's gracious acceptance of the apology, and the courage and humility he showed during this time, endeared him to the entire city. One editorial cartoon had a drawing of the Cardinal, with the phrase "Good guys wear black."

> *When I walked by the church on the afternoon of September 11, 2001, all three double doors were wide open, including the exterior and interior doors. Votive candles were placed around the altar beckoning the faithful to prayer. A special Mass was held that evening. It meant a great deal to me that Ascension was there for the community to come together in prayer on that awful day.*
>
> ✢ *Celine Woznica*

In June of 1995, the Cardinal was diagnosed with pancreatic cancer and underwent surgery. The surgery was thought to have been successful, but little more than a year later, the Cardinal learned that his cancer had returned. He spoke very publicly about how his illness changed his life and ministry. He appeared on the cover of national news magazines with the caption "Showing us how to die." He embraced a ministry to the sick, especially those suffering from cancer, and he conducted anointing liturgies throughout the archdiocese. He died on November 14, 1996.

When the Cardinal was diagnosed with cancer, the entire city opened their hearts to him. He knew he had their ear, and he spoke, taking full advantage of the opportunity to teach his flock. He urged people to strive for "real conversion of the heart for the sake

Bishop William McManus

It is common practice for a parish to request a certain bishop to administer the sacrament of Confirmation. It is rare, however, for that bishop to be a graduate of that parish's school. For many years, Ascension was fortunate to enjoy the presence of an honored alumnus, Bishop William McManus, at our Confirmation celebrations.

Each year that he presided at Confirmation, he arrived at least a half-hour early so that he could speak to the confirmands. He usually vested in front of them, explaining the meanings of the different pieces of a bishop's vestments—each one accompanied by a story from his past, some of which took place right here at Ascension.

After the Confirmation Mass and official reception, members of the parish staff often joined Bishop McManus in the rectory dining room, where he would regale us with wonderful stories of his experiences as priest, superintendent of schools, and bishop. It was like being in the presence of a living legend—sitting next to the man who signed every grammar school report card I had received. I was always impressed by his intelligence, his good humor, his genuine kindness, and his ready smile.

One year, we invited him to have dinner with the young men and women he had just confirmed. We served pizza and soft drinks, and he sat and talked with the teens. Smiling and laughing, he seemed to fit right in. At the end of the dinner, he turned to the students and said, "Will you pray with me?"

He called some of the students to stand with him. "Do you remember when I anointed you with the oil? Remember when I prayed, 'Send your Holy Spirit upon them to be their Helper and Guide. Give them the spirit of wisdom and understanding?'

How did you feel? What do you remember about that moment?" As they were now filled with pizza, he reminded them that they were also filled with the Holy Spirit. By being with them in this warm and unscripted way, he gave witness to how important they were.

The students responded to him, to his genuine concern and love for them. They expressed the fear they had felt prior to the ceremony, their awe during it, and the moments that genuinely moved them. This shepherd was able to draw out from them the most beautiful post-sacramental reflections I have ever heard. Perhaps, as he stood in the Pine Room, he was remembering his own Confirmation. Perhaps, as they stood there with him, they were aware of the future that awaited them.

Someone once said that if you started out to build the perfect bishop you would end up with William McManus. I think they were right.

Christine Ondrla
Director of Religious Education

of the poor and the needy." Ascension listened. It expanded the service work it was doing, the work that had been a hallmark of the parish for most of its existence.

The parish youth, already involved in service efforts, began to participate in the Appalachian Service Project (ASP), volunteering for a week of service in Appalachian communities each summer. Mark Breen was named the Director of Youth Ministry in 1997. Under his direction, the teen program flourished with social justice and service activities. Mark helped the entire community see the value in helping those outside our neighborhood. In 2002, twenty-nine people participated in Family ASP, a new program to aid the Appalachian community. Fifty-nine youth and twenty-four adults traveled to Appalachia for the summer project.

Praying in the spirit of Taizé. Photos by Micah Marty.

The parish continued its volunteer work with PADS and helped its sister parish, St. Martin de Porres, in particular, helping keep that parish's food pantry stocked with food. Parishioners formed a bereavement group to reach out to those grieving and, eventually, to assist in leading wake services. "Rainbows for All God's Children," a program for children who had experienced loss through death or divorce, ministered to Ascension's children. A Respect Life group emphasized pro-life outreach, prayer, and education and "adopted" pregnant women in need of support.

A Tradition of Justice

Building on Ascension's and Oak Park's history of inclusion, there were always groups in the parish to keep social justice issues on the table. Some forums included the "Building Bridges" workshop, the Peace & Justice and Social Ministry's Welfare Reform discussions, and Project Unity's "The Color of Fear." Backyard Theology presented arguments for the many ways of "being family," and Ascension School sponsored the "Tolerance Program." Father Jenks urged us "to move beyond family, Ascension, Oak Park—to all people who suffer humiliation and injustice." Ascension, along with three other parishes, hosted an ethnic sensitivity workshop at the Dominican Priory.

Parish Evaluation and Renewal

In 1998, the parish embarked upon a Parish Evaluation Project (PEP). Its goal was to help leadership develop a strategic plan for the immediate future and a clear vision of the distant future. Pastor Frank Jenks took great pride in the parish and in parishioners who, when called to help with the many and diverse ministries of Ascension, responded generously. Parishioners became Confirmation mentors, catechists, and prayer partners. They formed groups to welcome newcomers and to mentor engaged couples. C. J. Franklin, the pastoral associate beginning in 1995, began to explore the interests of young marrieds, young families, and young adults in the parish.

A New Cardinal

In May of 1997, Archbishop Francis George became Archbishop of Chicago; he would be named a Cardinal in January 1998. He began his service in the new role by meeting the people of the archdiocese in each of the respective vicariates; the gathering for our vicariate was held at St. Giles, where the Ascension choir sang at the celebration of the Eucharist.

Taizé prayer welcomes people of all ages and many Christian denominations to join in prayer. Photo by Micah Marty.

Cardinal George reached out to Chicago Catholics to help strengthen a church that was in danger of splintering. He held a Prayer Breakfast for Men and a Senior Unity Mass at Holy Name Cathedral and offered an ecumenical prayer service for persons living with HIV/AIDS and for those who care for them. George also celebrated a Remembrance Mass at Our Lady of the Angels for the fortieth anniversary of the tragic 1958 school fire. He offered his flock the opportunity to get to know him.

Christine Ondrla, Director of Religious Education, introduced the Catechesis of the Good Shepherd, a new program that began with four-to-six-year-olds and eventually expanded up to age twelve. Ascension's youngest students responded very positively to this Montessori-based program. In two years, Catechesis expanded from one session with twenty children to five sessions with seventy-six children.

The Ascension Women's Club, an organization that had taken the place of Ascension's Altar and Rosary Society, offered the first Morning

of Reflection for Women, which was attended by over 140 women. The AWC continued the Altar and Rosary mission of fundraising, community building, and offering spiritually sustaining programs for the women of Ascension. Young mothers started P.O.L.O. (Parents of Little Ones), and longtime parishioners started New Horizon for seniors.

Everyone in town was forming book groups in the 1990s, and Ascension started one of its own. Under the direction of the education commission, parishioners choose titles and lead discussions about their chosen books.

With the decrease in priests at Ascension, the parish reduced the number of weekday Masses to one per day in 1995. The 10:00 a.m. Sunday Mass was eliminated in 1998. The community that had gathered for that Mass continues to gather after the 9:00 a.m. Mass for "Extending the Word." Mass attendance at Ascension remained strong through the 1990s, although some in the community, with many other American Catholics, struggled with what some perceived as a more conservative bent to some of the church's leaders. The scandal and pain caused by the revelations of abuse by some priests caused the church to lose credibility with many people.

The 1990s were a time of trial for Ascension School, too. After the Ursulines left in 1986, the parish had a difficult time finding new leadership for the school. Tuition was up; enrollment was down. The school buildings were in bad shape. Controversies surrounding school staff discord led to a serious rift in the parish community, and Father Jenks broached the subject of closing the school. The School Board, challenged to save the school that had served the parish for more than eighty years, hired Mary Jo Burns, a high school administrator who had just become certified as a principal. Ms. Burns brought a wealth of experience with her, including service with the archdiocesan schools office, and began the project of board development immediately. With strong lay leadership supporting her and a core of dedicated faculty members, she rebuilt Ascension School, doubling enrollment in less than ten years. She made it possible for the community to look forward again with hope for the future of the institution.

In the late 1980s, Ascension School alumni formed an association, doing a tremendous amount of work to build and maintain a

> *Ascension is a spiritual home where I can enter the church and feel a sense of peace and relaxation.*
> ✢ *Eileen Pembroke*

database with contact information. The group held two very successful all-class reunions and collected more than two thousand names and addresses. The project became too large for even the most committed volunteers, though, and languished until the school opened a development office in 2001, with Lynn Fredrick as the director. With a development officer responsible for caring for alumni interests, the alumni association lent their database and their full support to the fledgling program, which soon began offering alumni events and outreach programs, and inviting alumni support of the school.

Physical Improvements

With the operations of the school in good hands, Father Jenks could look at the "big picture" for the parish, including the state in which we found our buildings. The physical plant was again in sore need of some attention. Pastoral Associate C. J. Franklin put on a hardhat for the role of facilities manager and, with the parish maintenance committee, oversaw several years' worth of projects, particularly in the school and church buildings. At the end of the school year in 1998, an army of volunteers emptied the first floor of the school. Contractors moved in and made the classrooms new, replacing ceilings and floors, windows, doors, and lockers. They installed new plumbing and electrical wiring, and prepared all classrooms for Internet access via cable. The following summer, the upper level was completed in the same way. Gradually, the school community replaced all the old school desks and outfitted a brand new computer lab.

The church received a new boiler, a new roof, and new gutters and downspouts. Tuck-pointing was done on the east parapet and the chimney. Windows were removed for cleaning and restoration work. The dome was covered with new copper.

Father Jenks and the parish finance committee had to find a way to pay for the work that was being done to "our old house." They signed on to Millennium 2000, an archdiocese-wide campaign, and followed it immediately with Sharing Christ's Gifts. For both efforts, the community of Ascension, with valiant educational work by parish leadership, stepped up to pledge their financial support to the work. Both campaigns were successful and the work was moving forward, but we were to find quite soon that there was more to be done and therefore more money to be raised. ✣

The Choirs of Ascension

Ascension Boys' Choir.

Since 1972, the Ascension Adult Choir has enriched the parish liturgies with beautiful singing. For many years, Ascension had a men's and boys' choir, directed by Mr. Al Trnka, with Mrs. Lorraine Thompson accompanying at the organ. In 1972, Sister Joan Ann Springman (Sister Immaculata), one of the Ursuline sisters who taught at Ascension School, was working for her Master of Music degree. She asked the people from Ascension who had sung in the chorus of the show *Cornz-a-Poppin'* to help her with her graduate recital, which took place at Grace Episcopal Church in Oak Park on July 23, 1972. Shortly after, Sue Weiland, who had replaced Al Trnka as organist/director, asked the group that had assisted Sister Joan Ann if they would sing for the celebration of Monsignor John Fitzgerald's fortieth anniversary of ordination, on Sunday, September 24, 1972. Their performance was impressive enough that they were asked to continue as the parish choir. On Thursday, September 28, 1972, the first rehearsal of the Ascension Adult Choir took place.

Ascension Adult Choir, 1979.

The choir, now known simply as the Ascension Choir, numbered around sixty members in the 2006–2007 season. The choir sings at 11:00 Mass on Sundays from late September through the end of the Easter season, except for the first Sunday of the month.

In 1993, under the direction of David Anderson, a second adult choir, the Ascension Schola, was formed. From an inaugural group of thirteen members, the Schola has become a fine choir, numbering a little more than forty members in the 2006–2007 season. They sing at the 9:00 Mass on the second and fourth Sundays of the month. Both choirs sing a repertoire of music drawn from different eras, styles, and cultures, all chosen to support and enhance the prayer of the people at liturgy.

In October 2001, about fifty members of the choir and an equal number of spouses, friends, and other pilgrims traveled to Italy on a musical pilgrimage. Because it was so soon after the attacks of September 11, 2001, there was some concern about traveling, but the choir decided to make the trip. Whatever fears there were about safety and

Ascension Choir and pilgrims at the Vatican, 2001.

political dissension soon disappeared under the warm welcome of the Italian people. Beginning in Baveno, a resort town on Lago Maggiore in the north of Italy, the tour progressed to Milan, Florence, Assisi, and finally to Rome for five nights. The choir sang brief performances in churches along the way and celebrated Mass in a small chapel in the Basilica of Saint Francis in Assisi with Father Frank Jenks presiding. In Rome, the choir sang at the Sunday celebration of the Eucharist at Saint Peter's Basilica and remained in Saint Peter's Square with hundreds of others to receive Pope John Paul II's blessing at noon from his balcony window. Later that evening, the choir gave a full concert, which was well received, at the Jesuit church of Saint Ignatius; the following Wednesday, everyone attended the general papal audience, at which the choir sang briefly.

Choir in concert at the church of Sant'Ignazio, Rome, 2001.

In July 2005, a pilgrimage choir, consisting of more than forty members of the Choir and the Schola, and spouses and pilgrims took a tour of Prague, Vienna, and Salzburg, which included singing at an evening weekday Mass at the Church of the Infant Jesus of Prague and at Sunday Mass at the Salzburg Cathedral (Mozart's church), on the eve of the Salzburg Music Festival. They also gave a brief concert at the Abbey of Melk and enjoyed a day or two of relaxation in the resort village of Garmisch. Of course, both tours included shopping, sightseeing, and sampling the local cuisines, wines, beers, and pastries.

On occasion, the choirs offer special performances. The Choir performed the *Requiem* of Gabriel Fauré in 1996 and *Requiem* by John Rutter in 1998, enhancing the November All Souls' Remembrances with music of consolation and comfort. In 1997, the choir was asked to sing at Cardinal Francis George's first Mass in Vicariate IV of the archdiocese. In 2001, the Choir offered a pre-pilgrimage concert, which was the same program that they would later perform in Rome. On May 18, 2007, the Choir and Schola gave a combined concert in celebration of the parish centennial.

The Choir also recorded *All Glory Is Yours* in 1998, and the Choir and Schola together recorded *Let Us Be Merry*, a collection of Christmas music, in 2004. Both CDs helped raise funds for the new Berghaus pipe organ, which was installed in the fall of 2004 and dedicated May 20, 2005.

The children's choir, begun in the late 1970s by Gina Orlando, continues under the direction of David Anderson as two choirs. The Choristers (Grades 5–8) sing on the first Sunday of the month at 11:00 Mass during the school year. They also sing on Holy Thursday at the Evening Mass of the Lord's Supper, where they participate in the procession of the Blessed Sacrament to the Altar of Repose and lead the singing of the *Pange Lingua*. The Cherub Choir sings at the "Children's Focus" Masses at 9:00 on the third Sunday of several months during the school year. In 2006–2007, about fifty children sang in each choir. Children from the parish school and religious education programs participate in both choirs. Like the adult choirs, the children's choirs are liturgical choirs; they sing to support and enhance the prayer of the entire assembly.

Each year, an Easter Vigil choir, made up of Choir and Schola members and others, is formed. The tradition of having a Good Friday Men's Choir, begun in the early 1980s by Julie Munaretto, continues.

Over the years, a few members of the Choir have become professional singers, and several current members are professional musicians. For all the adults and children who sing in the choirs at Ascension, learning and performing music expands the mind and heart. The members of the Choir and Schola often find that they joined the choir for the music and found a community as well. In lifting their voices to God together, a bond is formed. Members have rejoiced in each other's marriages, in the births and baptisms of their children, and in graduations, new jobs, and new homes; they have grieved when a member or a member's spouse or loved one died; they have supported each other in times of transition, illness, job loss, and other times of difficulty.

Ascension Choristers, 2005.

Berghaus organ, installed 2004.

late 1940s–early 1970s	Alois Trnka, Director
	Lorraine Thompson, Organist
1972–74	Sue Weiland, Organist/Director
early 1975	Sister Helen, Director
	Tom Stefan, Organist
1975–78	Gina Orlando, Director/Assistant Organist
	Tom Stefan, Organist
1978–79	Dr. Tim Bobinsky, Director
	Tom Stefan, Organist
1979–80	Tom Stefan, Director
	Russ Huette, Organist
1980–82	Julie Munaretto, Director
	Tom Stefan, Organist
1982–86	Julie Munaretto, Director
	Bob Mather, Organist
1986–88	David Anderson, Director
	Bob Mather, Organist
1988–90	David Van Sickle, Director
	Bob Mather, Organist
1990–	David Anderson, Director of Music, Organist
1992–	Elizabeth (Becky) Coffman, Associate Organist

Some information for this article was drawn from histories written by Jo Serio and Gina Orlando.

Youth Ministry at Ascension

Since the founding of Ascension Parish, young men and women have made significant contributions to the parish community. Their insight, energy, and passion have enriched and expanded Ascension's varied ministries.

A 1914 photo from the parish archives shows four beautiful young women—Gertrude and Agnes Shea, and Lillian and Leona Ann Mayo—bedecked in white dresses and oversized hair ribbons. Founding pastor Father Thomas J. McDevitt referred to them as "The Big Four." There are no records of how "The Big Four" earned their title from the pastor, but one can imagine that their youthful energy and leadership skills helped establish the fledgling parish. Indeed, five years later, Gertrude and Leona Ann entered the Ursuline order, the first two young ladies from Ascension Parish to become nuns.

Teens collecting for the homeless, 1991.

Prayer has always been a central part of youth ministry, and from the Young Ladies' Sodality of the early years to the Teen Masses of the later years, the youth of the parish have been able to celebrate their unique spirituality. Social life is also key in youth ministry, and dances, ski trips, open gyms, and other activities helped build teen community. In the 1950s, the teens were given their own space when the Canteen opened in the new school addition. (The Extended Day Program now uses the area.) The Canteen featured an ice cream parlor and was a popular gathering place for the Ascension young people, especially on Friday nights when the gym was reserved for teen roller-skating.

In the mid-1980s, youth ministry at Ascension entered a new phase when a laywoman, Sue Antoinette, joined the staff as a full-time youth minister. Sue had worked with Sister Felicia Wolff in the Religious Education office and soon began a parish outreach just to teens. In 1986, Sue organized the first Teen Takeover, a unique youth retreat experience that provided the teens a safe space to explore who they are and their relationship to God and to each other. The first Teen Takeover took place in one evening. Over the last twenty-one years, Teen Takeover has developed into a twenty-four-hour teen "lock-in" held in mid-March with a core leadership team and over 120 participants coming from area high schools. From Friday evening to the closing ceremony Saturday night, teens play, pray, sing, eat, talk, listen, reflect, and eat some more. What they don't do is sleep much. For many of the teens, Teen Takeover is such a profound and affirming experience that later, as college students and young adults, they return to help run the retreat.

Dan Woznica dancing with a Mexican child, 2004.

Two ASP (Appalachian Service Project) volunteers combine forces.

Erin Bracco with a lamb cake, April 2005.

Caroline Mason and a Mexican child share a moment, 2003.

The Teen Takeover Team, 1998.

Community service has always been part of the youth experience at Ascension, but in the 1990s, the initiation of weeklong youth service trips broadened the concept of community to Appalachia, and later to Tijuana, Mexico, and inner city Chicago. The first Appalachia Service Project (ASP) took place in summer of 1993 when three vans with fifteen teens and six adult volunteers left Ascension to drive to Kentucky. Fourteen years later, the service trip had twelve vans and over eighty adults and teens leaving Ascension's parking lot in June to make the trek to Appalachia. With the help of adult volunteers, the teens put their energy and muscle to make the homes in the area warmer, safer, and drier. Ascension teens have built wheelchair ramps, shored up sagging foundations, re-shingled roofs, installed bathrooms, and dug retaining walls for impoverished people in Appalachia. The effect of their work is not only felt by the beneficiaries of the project, but also by the teens themselves. For many of the teens, witnessing such poverty in the midst of the richest country in the world and barely a day's drive from their homes is a profound experience.

Ryan Mulvaney hammers a window frame in an Appalachian home.

Service trips to Tijuana, Mexico, began in summer of 1999. Although smaller in size because of transportation costs, these trips provide another opportunity for outreach to needy individuals and communities. As part of the Young Neighbors in Action (YNIA) youth ministry program, Ascension teens study Catholic Social Teaching and then put what they learn into action in various ministries of the Diocese of Tijuana. Teens have painted chapels, laid cement floors, run children's programs, worked in soup kitchens, and helped pass out food and clothing to poor families. A particularly moving experience for one group of teens was the construction of a small home out of cast-off garage doors for a family of ten. The teens became very close to the family over the week; when the home was completed, the teens used their own money to buy simple furnishings and bedding. Later, the entire youth group donated funds to help the family cover school fees and supplies for their children. For many of the teens, the trip to Tijuana is a chance to practice their high-school Spanish, but more importantly, it is an opportunity to gain insight into the social, economic, and political reality of the area.

Ascension Youth Ministry celebrates the unique gifts and energy of its young people and provides them with opportunities for prayer, community, leadership, and service. For many, the youth programs have shaped their lives. Many have returned to Ascension and are continuing the traditions of this great ministry. Others have entered full-time volunteer service after completing their education or have taken the skills they learned through youth ministry and applied them in other settings. Although youth ministry is about the teens' role in the Church of today, it does provide a glimpse of the Church of tomorrow. From what we have seen at Ascension, the future looks bright.

Dan Woznica and Kelsey Rosenquist work the back room at the Ascension Auction.

John McGuin, Bridget Morawski, and Edgar Woznica depart for the Katrina Hurricane Relief Trip, 2006.

CHAPTER EIGHT

Father Lawrence R. McNally

2003–Present

Father Jenks had served longer than the usual archdiocesan limit of two six-year terms at Ascension and left to become pastor of St. Alphonsus Parish, in Lemont. Cardinal Francis George named Father Lawrence R. McNally the ninth pastor of Ascension Parish; Bishop Jacobowski installed him in 2003. Father McNally, a Southside Chicago boy from a family that had already produced several priests, came to Ascension after serving as pastor at Queen of the Universe Parish. When the assignment became available, Father McNally visited Ascension "incognito," walking around the grounds and assessing the situation. He knew this was the parish for him and was thrilled when Cardinal George announced his appointment.

Father McNally made a memorable entry into the parish. His communication by letter in the *Dome* was detailed, personal, and expressive of gratitude. His presence was felt everywhere, both physically and emotionally. He met with all parish groups and appeared at all functions. He visited school classrooms daily and shared stories of his childhood, his priesthood, and his White Sox mania with the parish children. His energy, enthusiasm, warmth, and sense of humor (with puns as his humor of choice) quickly endeared him to all of Ascension.

Ms. Mary Jo Burns, principal, at the Pine Room opening.

Even an excellent pastor could not run the parish single-handedly. Father McNally expanded the pastoral staff and always gave credit to parish support staff who were here when he arrived, Rosemarie Nowicki, Mary Pat Landa, and Rose Hegarty, for the smooth working of the parish. He sought ways to take advantage of the Parish Pastoral Council and Commissions in leading the community. His personal approach to all parishioners invited even greater participation in parish ministries than before. Three men of the parish, Roger Vandervest (ordained in 2005), Lendell Richardson (ordained in 2006), and Joe Walsh (in formation), entered the Archdiocesan Diaconate Program. All were called to help, as the responsibility of "church" became that of the people.

During this time, the choirs of the parish recorded and released a second CD, this one featuring Advent and Christmas music, titled *Let Us Be Merry*, to help fund the building of the organ. A pilgrimage choir drawn from the parish choirs journeyed in 2005 to Prague, Vienna, and Salzburg.

Everything Old Is New Again

Although he had been told repeatedly not to make any big changes in the first year, Father McNally took a look at the Pine Room and said, "This is not acceptable." The Pine Room had been created by Father Ryan in the 1940s and desperately needed renovation. Pastoral Associate C. J. Franklin put on her project manager cap again and worked with contractors and the maintenance committee to renovate the center of Ascension's community life. The project grew, as these things do, when it was discovered that it would be necessary to excavate in order to correct plumbing problems under the school building. The work began at the close of the school year, with volunteers coming in to demolish the pine walls and the two ceilings: one tile and one tin. Workers tried to save the pine for memorabilia but found that it was far too dry for any use and therefore more of a fire hazard than had been known.

Opening lunch in the new Pine Room.

The Saint Francis of Assisi Meditation Garden.

With the Pine Room unavailable, the community struggled with schedules and special events for the first semester of the following school year. Daily school lunches moved into the gym balcony, and many special events that had traditionally been held in the Pine Room moved into the gym. Parishioners were invited into the gutted space and then came back again to watch the progress as the room took shape. They signed the concrete floor before the terrazzo was laid. School children drew pictures and wrote notes about current Ascension life for a time capsule that was placed behind the new Pine Room walls. Parishioners contributed with large and small gifts: the kitchen was dedicated to late parishioner Jerry Prete, following a gift by the Prete family; and other families donated to a fund that bought new folding chairs, new tables, a coffee maker, and a coat rack. The school alumni, who were solicited by the school for the first time, contributed over $80,000 for the work.

Donna Considine, Monica O'Meara, and Lendell and Tina Richardson bid at the Ascension School Auction.

Sox fans Grace Devitt and Olivia Gonzalez.

Father McNally and Ms. Burns calling for a "clean sweep" in the 2005 World Series.

The room was completed in January 2004. It was blessed by the parish, which moved back in with relief and gratitude for the new kitchen; the light; the elevator, which made the room accessible; the music studio; and the new bathrooms. Although the room no longer has pine paneling, it continues to be known as the Pine Room. Father McNally and Ms. Mary Jo Burns, the school principal, held a ribbon-cutting ceremony the first day that students returned to the Pine Room for lunch and treated the children to ice cream and cookies.

In the church, carpeting was removed to uncover the terrazzo floor. The rose window was restored, and in 2004, Berghaus Organ Company built a pipe organ, replacing the original Kilgen organ that had been installed when the church was built. The Village of Oak Park gave Ascension Parish the Historic Preservation Award for work completed on the exterior of the church and two floors of the school. But, as had come to be usual, there was more work before us. In the nineties, we had learned of some of the deterioration of our campus, but in the new

Easter Vigil 2007.

Catherine DeForrest, proud owner of a Mission Day fish.

Kristin Wirtz (center) and her young buddies, Maeve and Margaret Hillengas, at Mission Day 2006.

Chapter Eight: Father Lawrence R. McNally

Pat McAnany, Father McNally, and Deb Morawski help move the parish offices into the convent.

Char McAnany, moving day 2006.

millennium, additional life and safety issues were discovered. The rectory, having never quite recovered from its move in 1927, was unsound. Extensive deterioration of parts of the roof and the south wall led to the growth of mold in the walls; the electrical system was not safe. A decision to embark on major work on the church came with encouragement from the archdiocese: they were reluctant to insure the building any longer. A long-range building committee formed and sought a master plan for the next work on parish buildings.

A long-range plan is generally associated with a capital campaign, and, in spite of the fact that the parish had been through back-to-back campaigns, Ascension launched a third. Providing for Tomorrow sought to retire the debt remaining from six years of building projects, to allow for the purchase of the house next to the rectory as a "parsonage" for the pastor, and to outfit the convent for office and meeting space. Providing for Tomorrow helped lay the groundwork for Ascension's move to a stewardship model—one in which giving is not in response to need but in response to God's gifts in our lives. Parishioners hosted meetings for large and small groups; Father McNally laid out the case for the campaign. His enthusiasm and the sound business acumen of the parish finance committee helped the parish accept the plan.

Over the past several years, much work had been done throughout the parish plant, and some major maintenance work had been done to the exterior of the church. The time had come, just as the Centennial approached, to polish the interior of the church, the parish jewel. It had been fifty years since a complete painting of the church had been undertaken, and years of use and a small but smoky fire in January of 2005 had taken their toll.

Regina Art Glass workers restore the dome windows as part of the renewal of the church interior. Church work photos courtesy of Josh Hawkins and the Wednesday Journal.

Soon after graduation 2006, the work on the interior of the church began. The pews were removed and sent away to be refinished. The carpeting under the pews and the tile under the carpeting were removed, requiring the inside of the church to be tented for asbestos abatement. In July 2006, scaffolding was erected in the dome over a six-day period, and the painting of the church interior began. Folding chairs replaced the pews, a makeshift altar sat in front of the altar (and the scaffolding). Father McNally made a few memorable entrances at various Masses, descending the

Lisa Rigali Galvin was the principal designer of the 2006 interior painting project.

scaffolding from his hiding place in the dome. A few hearty souls climbed the scaffolding to get a close look at the new work and the old murals in the dome and the apse, which were kept and refurbished.

Chapter Eight: Father Lawrence R. McNally

Artists from Daprato-Rigali Studios discuss the apse mural.

Nervous brides (and their mothers) were concerned about how the structure would look in their wedding pictures but reported later that the scaffolding was not visible. It came down just in time for Christmas, and the pews returned, with plush new kneelers.

While this period saw the parish doing some important "housekeeping" work, not all the parish's energy was focused inward. The teens of Ascension's youth ministry and other adult leaders continued to build a program focused on serving others. Carwashes, flower sales, raffles, and stock investments raised the money necessary to support the Summer Service Projects in Appalachia and Tijuana. In 2002, twenty-nine people participated in Family ASP, a new venture to help the Appalachian community. Fifty-nine youths and twenty-four adults traveled to West Virginia and Virginia with ASP in the summer.

More Changes

In fall of 2004, Dan Lawler joined the staff as youth minister, followed a month or so later by Vicky Tufano, who succeeded C. J. Franklin as pastoral associate and later took on the added role of director of liturgy.

In June 2006, Tom Gull, the parish's first business manager, left his position but not the parish. He had established good business practices and processes in his nine years of service, serving the material aspects of the parish well so that its spiritual mission could be carried out. Later that year, Neil Heskin, an experienced parish business manager, joined the staff.

In August 2006, volunteers moved the parish offices from the rectory to the convent. The convent had not been in full use, other than a brief span as a retirement home, since the Ursulines had left Ascension School. The small rooms proved to be just the right size for offices, storage, and small meeting rooms. The maintenance committee, and, in particular, volunteers Bill Komala and Ann and Steve Devitt, cleaned and

painted, knocked down walls, and installed new lights and window treatments for the new offices. The building was rewired so that it could accommodate computers and air conditioners and the Internet. Father McNally blessed the "new" buildings following a Centennial Sunday Mass.

In September, Father McNally moved from his apartment in the rectory; it literally began to fall down around him. A group of investors from the parish had purchased the house next door to the rectory, 819 S. East, and it became the parish "parsonage" and a perfect home for the pastor. Plans began in earnest then for the next big change for the parish: the demolition of the rectory.

During the pastorate of Father Larry McNally, Ascension Parish completed its first century of life and faith by looking forward to the next one. The Centennial Committee, which included Father McNally, decided that the best way to mark the one-hundredth year would be to continue to live and pray as we do each year, as well as we can, mindful of the past, celebrating with a few special events in the present, and looking forward in hope. ✣

Chapter Eight: Father Lawrence R. McNally

A Tour of Ascension Church

Father McDevitt carried a dream of the church that would become Ascension Church ever since he saw a similar building during a trip to the Rhine River. Among the architecturally insignificant buildings on East Avenue, he wanted a strong classical facade of Romanesque-Byzantine style. He envisioned a portico with columns adorned by beautifully carved capitals (head stones). He asked for a copper dome of huge dimensions. When the architects, Meyer & Cook, warned him that such a building would collapse from the weight, the supportive arches and columns were added as a compromise. They now form the two side aisles on the north and south of the nave, with the vaulting giving the impression of a canopy of trees

The Facade

A facade is to a church much like what a face is to a person: it tells on the outside what is happening on the inside. The Ascension facade proclaims in large mosaic medallions of gold and blue, A.M.D.G.—*Ad Majorem Dei Gloriam*—to the Greater Glory of God. That is the motto; whatever Ascension people are doing within the church and, consequently, outside of the church walls, they are doing to the greater glory of God.

Seven statues, protected by colored glaze, have held up remarkably well for nearly eighty years in spite of exposure to extreme weather. They are Sts. Peter and Paul, the two great letter writers, martyrs, and founders of the Church; our two known protectors, St. Michael and St. Florian, guarding us against evil and the ravages of fire; and, in the center, a serene figure of Christ the King. Above this figure is the imposing Rose Window, which also has Christ the King as its focal theme. Next to the window are statues of Mary and of Joseph holding the Christ Child.

The Irish Cross forming the finial piece of the facade's gable, as well as the portico columns with their intricate carvings of St. Patrick themes, give honor to the Irish roots of the pastor and many of the founding families.

The Vestibule

From the East Avenue portal, one enters the vestibule. Originally, as the name suggests, a vestibule was to be used for the vesting of priests and ministers. Our vestibule, however, is very small and serves mainly to welcome the people as they enter and exchange a smile and a friendly word. The coats of arms of Pope Pius XI (1922–1939) and Cardinals Mundelein (1915–1939) and Stritch (1939–1958) over the vestibule doors are a link to the time of our founders.

The Nave

As you enter, the building delivers what it promises from the outside. There is perfect harmony between height and width, between the strength of the Romanesque arches and their noble expanse. Some church buildings can make us feel uncomfortable, while Ascension Church by its very architecture awakens all the right instincts in us. To indicate how completely we are united with Christ crucified and risen, the floor plan of the church was laid out as a Roman cross: one long vertical arm and one shorter horizontal arm intersecting the nave (the body of the church) at the four-fifths point.

The word "nave" is derived from the Latin word *navis*, the boat or the ship. The image of the church building as a boat, where all the people inside are safe and can face the outside dangers with confidence as long as Christ is with them, is strongly scriptural. It was typical of the time when our building was erected.

Ascension faces east (literally "oriented"), which is architecturally important as a symbol of the Church. Our orientation is Christ, our sun, and our rising light. We trust that, when our road is dark and confusing, Christ will send someone to us with his light to reorient us. We pray that we may be like Christ to others who need a ray of light. The colorful Rose Window emphasizes the orientation theme.

The Dome

The dome, which rises from where the cross arms of the building intersect, is our mark of distinction. As the glistening copper dome was being built in 1929, school children collected pennies with great enthusiasm so that the statue of Christ's Ascension could be placed on top. The structure was astonishing for its time, especially the lighting system, which was a first for a church in the country. Arranged on a movable track, the bulbs could be replaced while the attendant remained in the same position on the small gallery located at the base of the dome.

The Windows

As in other surrounding churches being built at the same time as Ascension, our precious stained-glass windows were designed, executed, and installed by Franz Mayer, Munich/New York. Our St. Magdalene window carries their signature. Associated then with the masterful Francis Xavier Zettler, the studio is now under the leadership of Dr. Gabriel Mayer and produces windows of ultramodern design that take your breath away.

At the time our church was built in 1929, their method of design was very well liked and accepted. They became famous for placing a most realistic scene of almost touchable present-day figures against a classical background. (See the heavy drapery, columns, and royal garments.) The art studio achieved outstanding perfection by employing only top-notch artists who specialized in certain areas. There were those who designed and executed nothing but the faces and hands in our windows, others worked only on flowers and greenery, and still others were exclusively responsible for the garments (a real splash of joyful colors).

Unlike medieval stained-glass windows where the scenes were composed of small chips of stained glass, our windows are painted. Onto the surface of colored glass is applied a fine emulsion of metal dust. Each pane of painted glass is then placed into a high-temperature oven, where the metal melts permanently into the glass and produces the detailed designs. When we wash our windows, the paint will never come off because glass and metal dust are permanently bound.

The entire production of stained glass is almost a miracle. Sand is mixed with different kinds of metal, either in the form of a powder or kernels, to produce the many shades of glass. Subsequently, the mixture is melted together in high-powered ovens. When a blob of semi-fluid glass develops, it is taken out of the oven and cooled by mouth blowing and turning on very long pipes until a cylinder-type bottle shape develops. This will be cut open when still warm and flattened. Only the cheap glass is mechanically produced. An enormous amount of lung-power has gone into our windows!

We are told that the themes of our Ascension windows did not follow a particular plan except for the Rose Window and the windows of St. Patrick (Irish founders) and St. Thomas Aquinas (Father Thomas McDevitt's patron saint). The art glass studio followed a tested pattern that was accepted then and still makes a lot of sense today: to pull together the history of the living Church, that is, Ascension worshipping and serving in the pews and in the homes and in the streets of Oak Park. They chose to create images of prophets, the fulfillment of the prophets, the Fathers of the Church whose theology and prayer forms have remained unsurpassed to this day, and the saints.

The prophets depicted in Ascension's windows are Joel and Aggaeus (Haggai), Nahum and Amos, Isaiah and Jeremiah, Baruch and Elias (Elijah), Zechariah and Habakkuk, Daniel and Hosea, Jonah and Abdias (Obadiah), and Ezekiel and Michaas (Micah). Their vision and prophecies are expressed in the two large transept windows showing the birth of the Savior and the child Jesus teaching in the temple.

The large windows in the side aisles are easily recognizable. They depict, on the north side, beginning at the crucifix shrine: St. Patrick, St. Gregory/Souls in Purgatory, Jesus and the children, the Wedding at Cana, and the Good Shepherd/Guardian Angel. On the south side, beginning at East Avenue: the Agony in the Garden/the apostles sleeping, Peter receiving the keys to heaven, Our Lady of Lourdes appearing to Bernadette, and Pentecost. The last large window before the transept shows Mary Magdalene washing the Lord's feet.

All the windows are self-explanatory except for one, the second on the northeast side, called "The Mass of St. Gregory." History has called him The Great. He was pope from 590 to 604 AD and was influential in renewing and unifying the liturgy. The Gregorian chant is named after him. This great organizer was gifted with mystical experiences, such as seeing Christ on the cross and conversing with him while celebrating the Mass. In this window can be seen souls leaving Purgatory as one of the fruits of the Mass.

The saints are, beginning at the choir loft on the north side (Van Buren Street): St. Cecilia, St. Joan of Arc, St. Ursula, St. Angela (patroness and foundress of our Ursuline Sisters), St. Rose of Lima, St. Agnes, St. Therese, St. Anne, St. Elizabeth, and St. Catherine of Siena. The procession of saints continues on the south side with male saints. Beginning at the choir loft they are: St. David, King; St. Edward, King; St. William, King; St. Anthony; St. Francis of Assisi; St. Malachy; St. Stanislaus; St. Aloysius; St. Alphonsus of Liguori; and St. Thomas Aquinas.

The Walls, Ceiling, and Floors

In celebration of the fiftieth anniversary of the founding of Ascension Parish, the church was repainted. The ceiling murals and symbols in the triforium were also changed at this time. The murals in the dome are actually not what one usually calls a mural, that is, a painting on the wall. Our "murals" were done on canvas in the artist's studio and then carried up on extremely high scaffolds and applied to the dome's ceiling with glue. Angelo Gherardi of Park Ridge, the artist who designed and executed the paintings, told this story: He and his co-workers of the Daprato-Rigali Studios had just pasted the canvas to the ceiling under extreme efforts at nauseating heights when they broke for lunch. As they returned, the paintings were gone. They had torn loose from the weight of the canvas and wet glue and were lying crumpled on the floor. What horror! Fearing that the canvas would be torn and the paint cracked and endless hours of artistic work would have been in vain, they found to their utter surprise that the paintings were undamaged.

At the same time, carpet layers were applying floor covering to the terrazzo flooring of the church. They suggested that their tar-like "sure-stick" carpet glue would support the canvas as well. Gherardi took their advice. He never returned to Ascension Church until he attended our Golden Jubilee Mass on October 7, 1979, but he did not want to look at the ceiling for fear that black blotches of tar had seeped through the canvas. This possibility had haunted him in dreams for a long time.

In preparation for the parish centennial, the entire church was repainted in 2006 by Daprato-Rigali. The carpeting, which had earlier been partially removed, was completely removed and replaced with tile. The pews were refinished. The original terrazzo in the aisles and sanctuary continues to add beauty to the church.

The Liturgical Furnishings

Following Vatican II, the altar was brought forward and placed under the great dome to conform to the new liturgical norms. At first, it was a wooden altar on a wooden platform. The present altar was erected in the early 1970s. It is a marble mensa (altar table top) resting on four decorated marble posts of the former altar rail, all on a marble platform. The same mosaic inlay connects the altar with all the other mosaic ornamentation in the building and makes it look harmonious, as if it had always been there. At this same time the present altar was built, the lower half of the church was repainted (and again in 1993) and carpeting was installed. The pews in the apse were repositioned at this time as well.

In any church there are several focal points: the altar where Christ becomes present in the Eucharist; the lectern (ambo or pulpit are other words for it) where God becomes present when the Word is being read, heard, interpreted, and accepted by the faithful; the person of the priest leading the assembly in prayer and, as Christ's representative, offering Christ's sacrifice to God for our salvation; and the baptismal font, the place of entry into the Church.

At Ascension, these powerful concepts are well applied. The altar is closely surrounded by the people, the pews in the transept have been turned to face the altar and each other so that we can see and encourage one another by our communal prayer, our singing, and our devout concentration on the Lord. The priest's chair closes the circle of seating. He sits not on a throne but in a pew, just as we do. Although his function is different from ours, he is essentially part of the assembly.

The former high altar has remained unchanged except for its primary function. It houses the tabernacle, which holds the sacred bread. Above the tabernacle rises a baldachino with blue and gold and colorful mosaics. They represent a view of heaven, of paradise, of the Garden of Eden, where nature is ordered.

The Organ

The Kilgen Organ Company, St. Louis, Missouri, built the original organ in 1929. It had three manuals and twenty-three ranks of pipes. In late 2004, Berghaus Organ Company, Bellwood, Illinois, replaced it with an organ of three manuals and forty ranks. In early 2005, a small fire in the ushers' room of the church created a great deal of smoke. After being cleaned and voiced, the organ was dedicated on May 20, 2005.

Dates and Measurements

Cornerstone: Laid Easter Sunday, 1929, and blessed by Father Francis A. Ryan, who would become the third pastor of Ascension in 1944.

Church Dedication: January 15, 1930

Exterior dimensions of the church: 92′ wide by 162′ long
Floor of the church to the top of the dome: 100′
Ascension of Christ statue atop the dome: 15′
Interior diameter of the dome: 32′
Altar platform beneath the dome: 16′
Main aisle: 100′
Rose Window: 16′ in diameter
Windows in lower half of church: 5 1/2′ by 10′
Clerestory windows: 4′ by 7′
Windows in apse: 11′ by 15′

Regina Kuehn
Parishioner, Artist,
Liturgical Design Consultant

Ascension opened its centennial year on June 25, 2006. Bishop Thomas Paprocki was the main celebrant at a Mass concelebrated by Father Larry McNally, Father Bob Cross, Father Larry Schmuhl (uncle of Father McNally), and Father Frank Jenks.

CHAPTER NINE

The Centennial Year

2006–2007

Ascension opened the celebration of the centennial year on June 25, 2006, with a beautiful Mass. Bishop Thomas Paprocki was the main celebrant; Father McNally, his uncle Father Larry Schmuhl, Father Robert Cross, and Father Frank Jenks concelebrated. The youth of the parish returned from a service trip to Appalachia just in time to process into the church for an end-of-Mass blessing. It was a moving moment: the future of our parish coming home from having served others, in order to start our *next* hundred years!

A block party followed. Banners in the neighborhood proclaimed the news of our celebration and the support of local businesses. Current and returning parishioners were invited to record their memories for posterity. They also ate bratwurst, played games, and listened to music.

The Ascension Centennial year was not one of a busy parish pausing to look back. There was no pause, and at least as much looking forward as there was looking back. A committee helped to shape the events of the year, finding it difficult sometimes to find time that wasn't already scheduled with Ascension events. Another group began to gather information, stories and photographs about our history, to share with the community, building archives as they went along.

Deacon Lendell Richardson proclaims the gospel at the opening Mass of the Centennial Year, June 25, 2006.

Throughout the year, children and adults of the parish were asked what they think Ascension will be like in the next one hundred years. Their imaginations included children jet-packed to school and a stream in the sanctuary for baptisms. Parishioners gathered for Centennial Sundays monthly, enjoying the exhibits created by members of the Centennial committee and munching on doughnuts.

In April, the centennial dinner dance was held at the Doubletree Hotel in Oak Brook. Over four hundred current and past parishioners celebrated together at an elegant dinner and danced to music from our history. One parishioner said of the event, "It was a combination of wedding, class reunion, and block party, everyone with this one great thing in common: our love for Ascension."

Parish teens were welcomed back from their service in Appalachia.

    The combined choirs of the parish presented "One Hundred Years of Song," on May 18, a beautiful and ambitious concert of sacred music. Former music directors, organists, and musicians joined the audience in the packed church to savor the talent of our own.

    On Ascension Sunday, May 20, 2007, Cardinal Francis George, although recovering from a broken hip, presided at the concelebrated Mass with the current and previous pastors and other priests who had served our community. The music for the liturgy of the day was joyful, topped off with the assembly standing to sing the "Te Deum," the traditional hymn of praise, in its best-known setting, "Holy God, We Praise Thy Name." A grand reception in the gym followed, bringing a close to the Centennial Year. ✛

Bishop Thomas Paprocki

Centennial block party fun.

Bishop Paprocki joined Ascension parishioners at the block party following the opening Mass.

Many, many sweet things at the Centennial block party.

Children and teens enjoyed the climbing wall.

Chapter Nine: The Centennial Year

Claudia Hallissey and Mary Ellen Chwedyk enjoyed listening to Fr. Bob Cross's stories as he recorded them at the Centennial block party.

Winifred Halvorsen Soucie ('33) and classmate Bill Kevil reminisce as Keith Kalemba records their memories.

Father Larry McNally dedicates the convent as the new Parish Center.

Chapter Nine: The Centennial Year

What Will Ascension Be Like in a Hundred Years?

We learned a lot in the last hundred years. We will have fun learning more about Jesus and Mary in the next hundred years. I'll like the church no matter how old it gets because that's God's home!

Brooke Lynch
Second grader

In the future, I will make sure all the children are safe in the courtyard. Gates will be rusty; by then the rectory would have fallen down. Ascension people are good at cleaning things up and building new things. Ascension will still be the best parish ever!

Chris Kambach
Second grader

It will have a stream in the middle of church with angel fish in the water. There will be a yellow bridge going side to side. Babies would be baptized in the stream making it more like when Jesus was baptized by John the Baptist.

John Marchand
Third grader

The Truth is immutable. The Creed will be unchanged. The liturgy and social functions will probably adapt to technology and demographics.

Pat and Bill McNichols

It will be centered in a "high density" community—really an extended city of Chicago. It will require continued preservation. It will be preserved because it will be loved.

Victor and Nancy Rodriguez

Who knows? I hope all the trials the Church has had lately will be over, and we will still be a solid institution for the times.

Mary Deady

Who knows, but God will be in charge, not us! I really believe that.

Bob Connelly

The parish Lenten mission focused on the art and theology of the St. John's Bible.

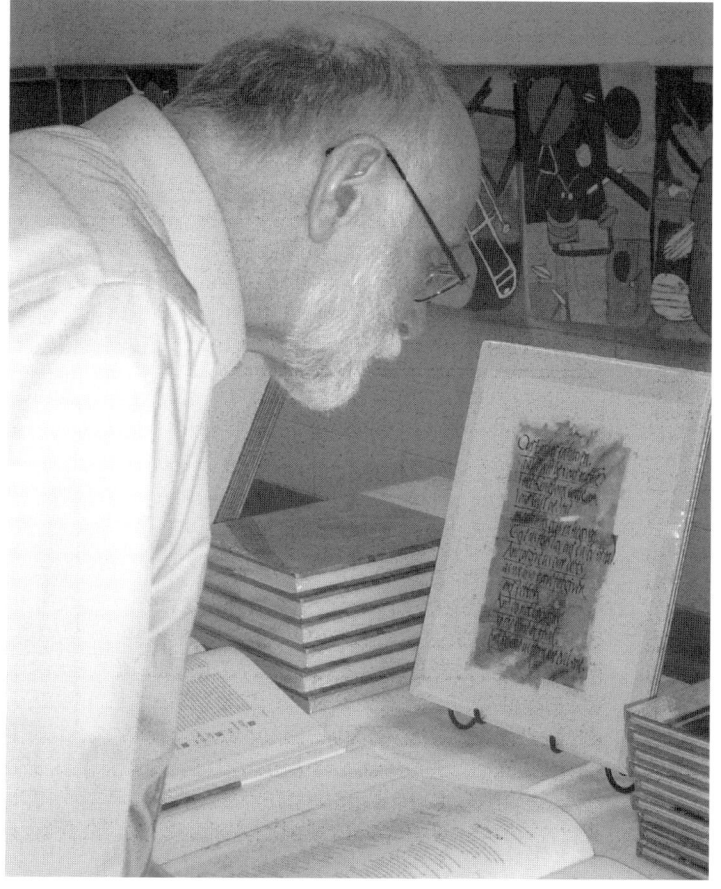

Children participated in the Lenten mission by creating their own illuminated manuscripts.

Chapter Nine: The Centennial Year

Mildred McDonald toasts Ascension at the Centennial dinner dance, April 2007.

Table 28 enjoys a laugh at the Centennial dinner dance.

Tina and Lendell Richardson, Roger Vandervest, and Kathy and Joe Walsh, present and future deacons at Ascension, celebrate at the dinner dance.

Mike Clark and Father Hal Stanger share a moment at the Centennial dinner dance.

Chapter Nine: The Centennial Year

Father McNally welcomes Cardinal George to Ascension for the concluding liturgy of the Centennial Celebration on May 20, 2007.

Father Larry McNally and Father Bill Burke.

The Ascension Choir and Schola offered a concert, One Hundred Years of Song, on May 18, 2007.

Jacob Gregory led the assembly in the responsorial psalm.

Chapter Nine: The Centennial Year

Cardinal Francis George preached the homily.

Chapter Nine: The Centennial Year

Mary Lou and John Dwyer reminisce with Fr. Jerry Joyce at the reception following the Centennial closing Mass.

Father Larry McNally shares a moment with longtime parishioners.

Chapter Nine: The Centennial Year

Ascension Parish Centennial Prayer

Eternal God,
through his Ascension,
your Son Jesus Christ went before us
to prepare a place for us
and to take his seat at your right hand.

The family of Ascension
comes before you with thanks
for our ancestors in faith,
who established this parish one hundred years ago
and for all who have followed them through the years
to make this a place
where your love is proclaimed,
your ways are taught,
your praises are sung,
and your people serve and are served.

May we be mindful of all that you have done for us.
May we be grateful for your many blessings to us.
May we be hopeful that your great love will continue to guide us
until we come with joy to the place prepared for us.

This we pray in the name of Jesus,
who lives and reigns with you in the unity of the Holy Spirit,
one God forever and ever.
Amen.

Ascension Centennial Fund Donors

The Founders' Society

Tom & Tracy Brooker

James & Kathleen Carney
In memory of Michael E. Carney

Paul Gearen

Beatrice Gibbons
In memory of Patrick Gibbons

Thomas Gull & Tim Flesch

Stephen & Mary Jo Herseth

Eugene & Cecilia Masella
In memory of Peggi Masella Poole

Rev. Lawrence McNally
In memory of Robert & Mary Jane McNally

Frank & Eileen Muriello
In honor of the Muriello Family

Jack & Rosemarie Nowicki

Neil Pembroke & Eileen McFadden

Greg & Lisa Peters

Roy & Frances Picone

Mary Jo & Stephen Schuler

The Domers' Society

Bob & Mary Jean Connelly
In memory of Elizabeth McAvoy

John & Kay Duff
In memory of Susan Duff '69

Don & MaryBeth Granholm

Jack & Rosemary Joyce
In honor of the Walker & Hopkins Families

Karen & Bill Komala

Joseph McDonald & Madeleine Raymond
In memory of Mary Mullen McDonald

Sue & Mike Quinn

James & Kay Wallace

Don & Celine Woznica

The Pastors' Society

Mary Eileen Ryan Altier

Roberta Arnold

Al Belanger

Colleen & Dennis Bracco

Fred & Mary Beth Brandstrader

Donald & Judy Breezer

Kenny & Jennifer Burns

Ken & Kathy Cliff

Jack & Nancy Coaker
In memory of Jack & Jean Sweeney

Jim & Kay Costello
In honor of the Costello & Flaherty Families

David & Barbara Dries

Kevin & Julie Duff

Dick Dunne

Ed Duthaler & Barb Harmon

John Englehart

The Kane Family
In memory of Robert J. & Thomas Kane

Margaret & Wilson Lee

Bill & Patricia McNichols
In memory of Mary & James McNichols

Nancy Quinn

Marie Wackrow
In memory of Edward & Gerald Wackrow

Chris, Grace & Cassidy Winston

The Centennial Society

The Bennett Family
In memory of Bud Bennett

Richard A. Bingen
In memory of John & Katherine Moore

Robert Bransley

Mary Jane Joyce Byrne

Valerie M. Chathas

Martin Costello

John Deeming
In memory of Richard Kutz

Stephen & Ann Devitt

Dan Dobruse & Sue Tindall

Joan Dunn

Oscar & Aida Feliciano
In honor of Terrado & Feliciano Families

Tic & Kathy Flannery

James & Lynn Fredrick

Mark & Sheila Gartland

Michael & Connie Gill

Judy & Tom Gyland
In memory of Ann Jablonski

James Haley

Ascension Centennial Fund Donors

Ms. Mary L. Haley

Leo & Kathleen Harmon

Mary Therese Lamb Hilan

David & Suzanne Holmes

Tom & Donna Ioppolo

Willie & Mitzi Irons

Emil & Carol Kane

Tom & Norine ('42) Kresich Slott
In memory of Mother Florentine, OSU

The Kuehn Family
In memory of Heinz Kuehn

Sam & Ann LaGuardia

Tom & Mary Pat Landa

Paul & Gussie Lenehan

Leo & Linda Lewis

Linda Marcangelo
In memory of Mary B. Marcangelo

Fred & Pat Martin

Margaret M. McCarthy

The McEachen Family
In memory of Cecelia McEachen

John M. McHugh

Virginia Meyers
In honor of the Doyle/Sheehy Families

Margaret Mlady
In honor of the Mlady-Houha-Mayo Families

Marilyn Trnka Mozockie

Edward & Carol Mulvihill
In memory of Rose & Sam Dewbray

Thomas Muriello

New Horizon

Tom & Meg Northey

Jean Ott

Leo & Estelle Pargulski

Betty Puchalski

Paul & Kate Seavey
In memory of Mary Jean Connelly

Clement & Alicia Simon

Dick & Louise Snyder

The Sorenson Family

Richard & Patti Spangler

Felicito & Elena Sugay

Kathleen Sweeney
In memory of the deceased members of the Phillip Sweeney Family

Steve & Rosemary Talianko

Marilyn & Ken Trainor
In honor of the Trainor Family

Michael & Mary Ucinski

Ed & Mary Waadt
In memory of Stella Waadt

Edward Walsh

Bernard L. Wise
In memory of Irene Wise

Leo & Alicia Yaus
In memory of Mary Jean Connelly

Margaret Zangrilli
In memory of Joseph F. Zangrilli

The Ascension Society

Dave Adams & Mary McEnery

Sam Amato
In memory of Thomas & Patricia Murphy

Dolores AuBuchan Hansen

Michelle Barton & William Zbierski

Charley & Kathy Bennett & Family
In honor of Mary & Bud Bennett

Timothy & Mary Beth Blatner

William Bobco

Ascension Centennial Fund Donors

Marjorie Boland '43 & Mary Bennett '64

Linda Brozeau-Moss

Mary Jo Burns

Mary Deady

Eileen Dempsey-Grace

Steve & Margaret Durante & Family
In honor of Mary & Bud Bennett

John & Mary Lou Dwyer

Judith Eisenmann

Shirley E. Esenther

Frank & Kathleen FioRito

Peggy Gawne
In memory of William J. Gawne

Sam Harnish & Mary Jo Wenckus

Roy & Margaret Heinekamp
In memory of Mary V. Reichenback

Bernice Hopkinson-Juettner

Anthony J. Iannantuoni
In memory of Marilyn Iannantuoni

Catherine Jacobs

Jim & Sue Janssen & Family
In honor of Mary & Bud Bennett

Margret M. Kelly

Donald & Eleanor Kraft

H. Faye Kutz
In memory of Richard J. Kutz

Marjorie Long

Robert & Bonnie Mather

McCluskey Family
In honor of Mary & Bud Bennett

Anne Murphy
In memory of Dick Murphy

Margaret Noak

Mary Helen (Bennett) Novak & Family
In honor of Mary & Bud Bennett

Ed & Mary O'Brien
In memory of Walter & Mary Magrady

Dennis & Fran O'Brien

Mary O'Connell

Hedy Pajonk

Gina Petruzzelli-Reckard

Anne Prete

John & June Quirk

Eileen Regan

Irene Sanduski

Mary Jane Schenn

Judith I. Sheehy

Joseph & Kathy Walsh

Eugene & Angela White

Mary Wojcik & Jim Wojcik

We are deeply grateful to all our donors. We apologize for any errors or omissions.